CADERNO do Futuro

A evolução do caderno

LÍNGUA INGLESA

Book 1
ENSINO FUNDAMENTAL

3ª edição
São Paulo - 2013

IBEP

Coleção Caderno do Futuro
Língua Inglesa – Book 1
© IBEP, 2013

Diretor superintendente	Jorge Yunes
Gerente editorial	Célia de Assis
Editor	Angelo Gabriel Rozner
Assistente editorial	Fernanda dos Santos Silva
Revisão	André Odashima
	Rachel Prochoroff
Coordenadora de arte	Karina Monteiro
Assistente de arte	Marilia Vilela
	Nane Carvalho
	Carla Almeida Freire
Coordenadora de iconografia	Maria do Céu Pires Passuello
Assistente de iconografia	Adriana Neves
	Wilson de Castilho
Ilustrações	José Luís Juhas
Produção gráfica	José Antônio Ferraz
Assistente de produção gráfica	Eliane M. M. Ferreira
Projeto gráfico	Departamento Arte Ibep
Capa	Departamento Arte Ibep
Editoração eletrônica	N-Publicações

CIP-BRASIL. CATALOGAÇÃO-NA-FONTE
SINDICATO NACIONAL DOS EDITORES DE LIVROS, RJ

K38i
3.ed.

Keller, Victoria
    Língua inglesa : book 1, (6º ano) / Victoria Keller, pseudônimo dos autores Antonio de Siqueira e Silva, Rafael Bertolin. - 3. ed. - São Paulo : IBEP, 2013.
    il. ; 28 cm   (Caderno do futuro)

    ISBN 978-85-342-3568-6 (aluno) - 978-85-342-3572-3 (mestre)

    1. Língua inglesa (Ensino fundamental) - Estudo e ensino. I. Título. II. Série.

12-8683.   CDD: 372.6521
                                      CDU: 373.3.016=111

27.11.12   03.11.12   041074

3ª edição - São Paulo - 2013
Todos os direitos reservados.

IBEP

Av. Alexandre Mackenzie, 619 - Jaguaré
São Paulo - SP - 05322-000 - Brasil - Tel.: (11) 2799-7799
www.editoraibep.com.br editoras@ibep-nacional.com.br

CTP, Impressão e Acabamento

SUMÁRIO

CONTENTS

LESSON 1 – ABOUT YOU	4
LESSON 2 – ENGLISH IN THE WORLD	7
LESSON 3 – ARTICLES	9
REVIEW	13
LESSON 4 – VERB TO BE: VERBO SER OU ESTAR	14
LESSON 5 – IS SHE A TEACHER?	22
LESSON 6 – INTRODUCING PEOPLE	26
REVIEW	30
LESSON 7 – DEMONSTRATIVES	33
LESSON 8 – MEETING PEOPLE – I	37
LESSON 9 – MEETING PEOPLE – II	44
LESSON 10 – WHERE ARE YOU FROM?	48
REVIEW	52
LESSON 11 – IMPERATIVE - AFFIRMATIVE FORM	55
LESSON 12 – IMPERATIVE - NEGATIVE FORM	58
LESSON 13 – DIFFERENT BEDROOMS	64
LESSON 14 – IS THAT YOUR HOUSE?	69
REVIEW	72
LESSON 15 – PREPOSITIONS OF PLACE	75
LESSON 16 – NUMBERS	79
LESSON 17 – HOW MANY...?	81
LESSON 18 – HOW MUCH...? HOW MANY...?	83
LESSON 19 – HOW OLD ARE YOU?	86
REVIEW	89
LESSON 20 – WHAT TIME IS IT? – I	92
LESSON 21 – WHAT TIME IS IT? – II	93
ADDITIONAL TEXTS	95
FUN TIME – DIVIRTA-SE APRENDENDO	108
GENERAL VOCABULARY	114

SUBJECT

NAME

TEACHER

	MONDAY	TUESDAY	WEDNESDAY	THURSDAY	FRIDAY	SATURDAY	SUNDAY
HOUR							

TESTS AND WORKS

Lesson 1 – About you

1. About you:

a) What is your name?

_____

_____

b) How old are you? I am _____ years old.

c) Where were you born? I was born in _____

d) Are you tall or short?
I am _____

e) What color are your eyes?
( ) brown ( ) blue
( ) black ( ) green

f) What color is your hair? (blond, red, brown, black)
My hair is _____.

2. Your address:

a) Where do you live?
I live at _____
              (number)

_____
(street, avenue)

_____   _____
(ZIP Code)   (town)

_____   _____
(state)   (country)

b) What is your telephone number?
My telephone number is

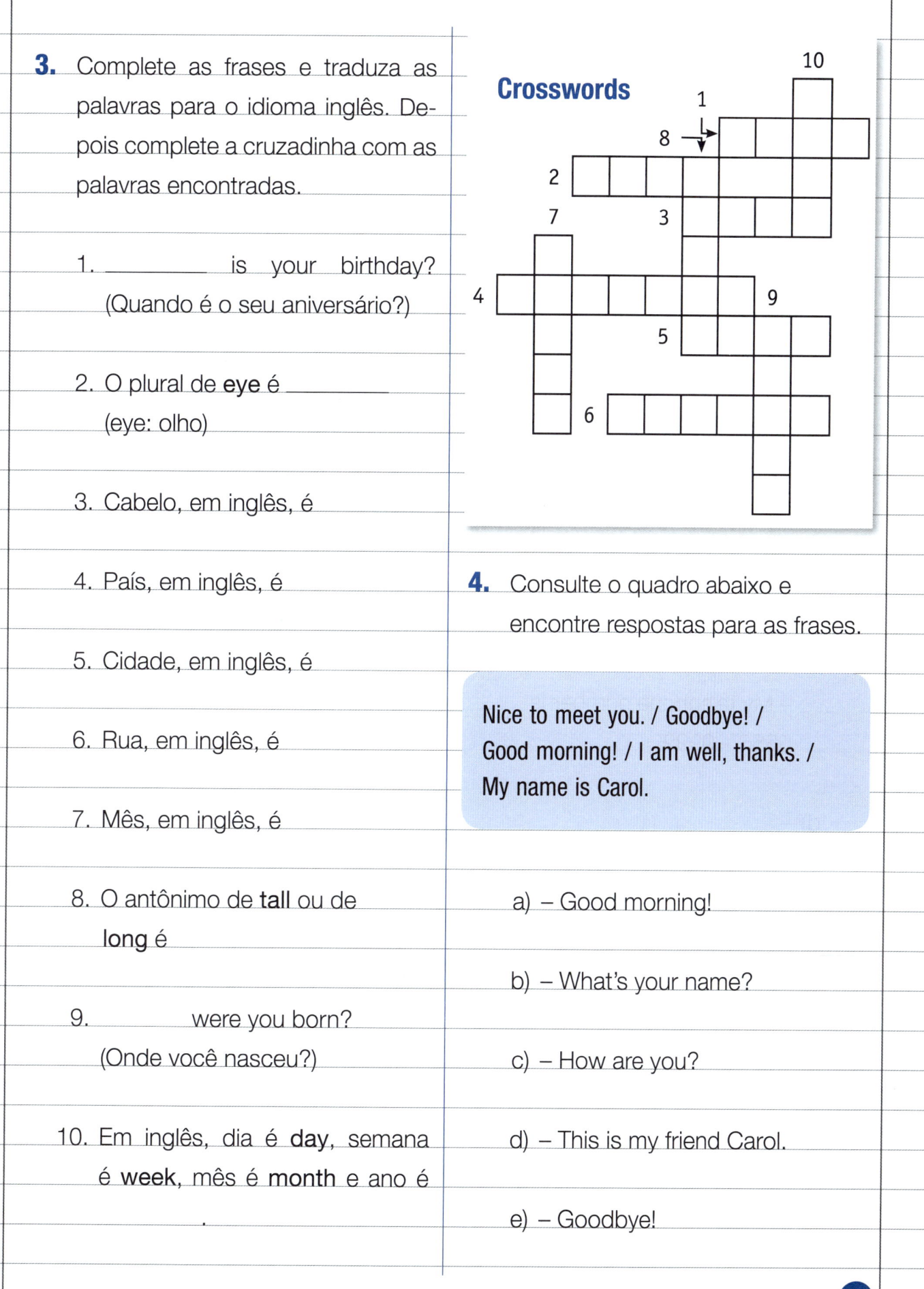

3. Complete as frases e traduza as palavras para o idioma inglês. Depois complete a cruzadinha com as palavras encontradas.

Crosswords

1. _____ is your birthday?
   (Quando é o seu aniversário?)

2. O plural de **eye** é _____
   (eye: olho)

3. Cabelo, em inglês, é

4. País, em inglês, é

5. Cidade, em inglês, é

6. Rua, em inglês, é

7. Mês, em inglês, é

8. O antônimo de **tall** ou de **long** é

9. _____ were you born?
   (Onde você nasceu?)

10. Em inglês, dia é **day**, semana é **week**, mês é **month** e ano é _____ .

4. Consulte o quadro abaixo e encontre respostas para as frases.

Nice to meet you. / Goodbye! / Good morning! / I am well, thanks. / My name is Carol.

a) – Good morning!

b) – What's your name?

c) – How are you?

d) – This is my friend Carol.

e) – Goodbye!

5. Complete o diálogo fazendo as perguntas que estão no quadro abaixo.

- What color are your eyes?
- What is your telephone number?
- How are you?
- Where do you live?
- What is your name?

First name: Paul
Last name: Parker
Age: 11 years old
Date of birth: 25/10/1986
Address: 14 Florida Street - Brooklyn
Class number: 01
Teacher's name: Sylvia
Parents' names: Margaret Parker, John Parker
My friends' names: Peter, Mary and Jim
Telephone numbers: (home) 555-5555
(cell phone) 999-9999

a) –
   – I am fine.

b)
   – My name is John.

c)
   – My telephone number is 5555 – 9999.

d) –
   – My eyes are blue.

e) –
   – I live at 25 Copacabana Street.

Registration form

6. Veja o modelo e preencha a ficha com os seus dados pessoais:

First name:

Last name:

Age:

Date of birth:

Address:

Class number:

Teacher's name:

Parents' names:

My friends' names:

Telephone numbers:
(home) _____
(cell phone) _____

Lesson 2 – English in the world

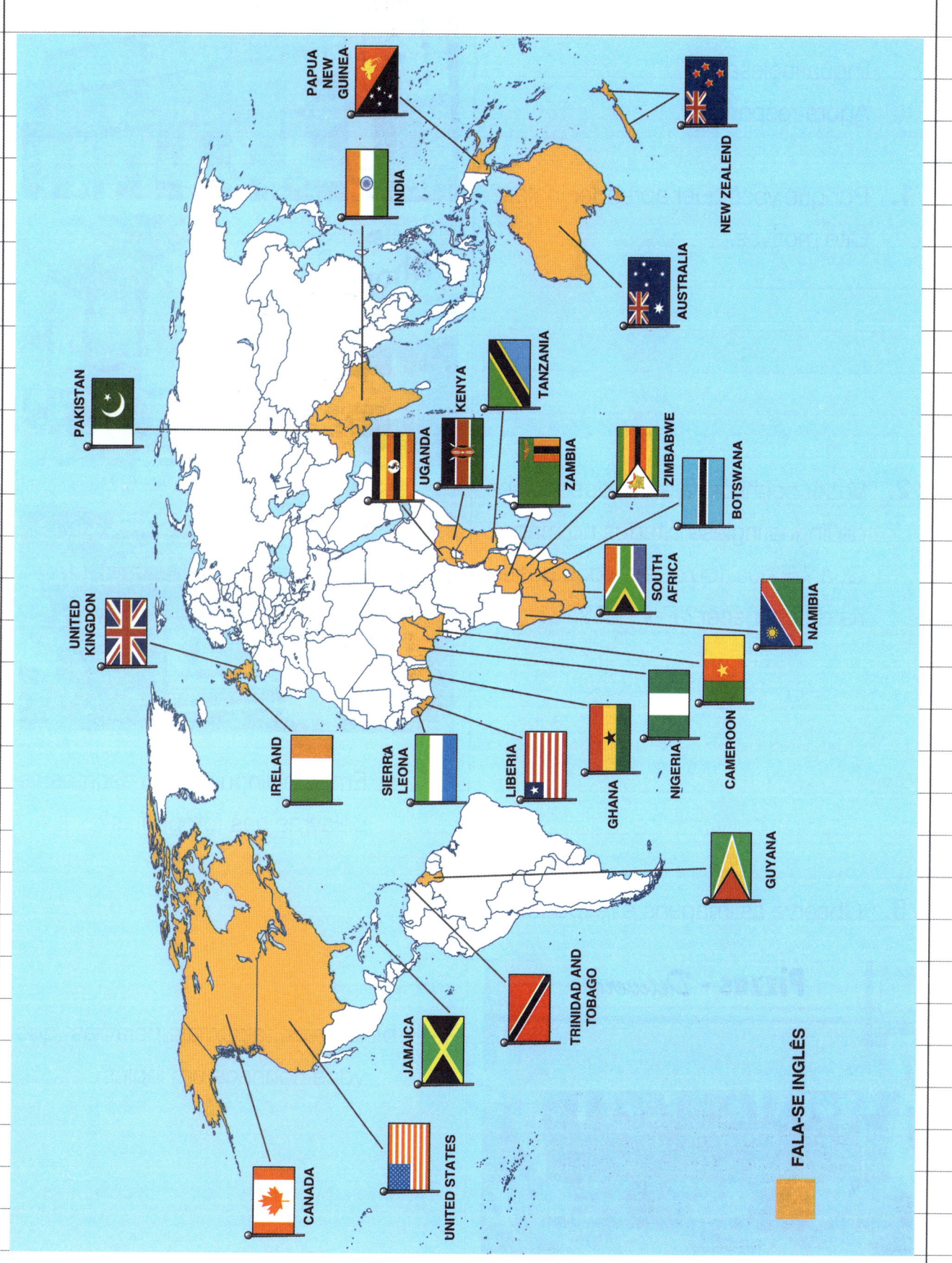

Observe o mapa e veja alguns países do mundo onde se fala a língua inglesa.

Agora responda:

1. Por que você quer aprender inglês? Cite motivos.

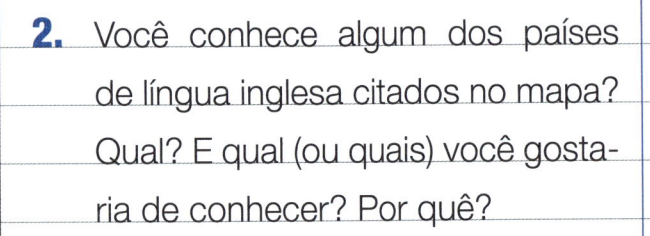

2. Você conhece algum dos países de língua inglesa citados no mapa? Qual? E qual (ou quais) você gostaria de conhecer? Por quê?

a) Em qual língua estão escritas as palavras nas fotografias?

3. Observe as imagens e responda:

b) Escreva algumas palavras que você conhece em inglês.

Lesson 3 – Articles

> Dad, look **a** flying saucer!

> It's not **a** flying saucer, son. It's **a** building designed by **an** architect called Oscar Niemeyer.

ARTICLES (ARTIGOS)

1. **Definido:**

   the – É invariável e significa "o, a, os, as":

   the boy, the boys, the girl, the girls.

2. **Indefinido:**

   a – Usa-se **a** diante de palavras que começam com consoante ou **h** aspirado:

   a cat, a boy, a hospital, a hat.

   an – Usa-se **an** diante de palavras que começam com vogal e **h** mudo:

   an animal, an apple, an hour.

   Não se usa artigo indefinido no plural:

   a boy → boys;

   an animal → animals.

   (Forma-se o plural dos substantivos, em inglês, geralmente acrescentando-se um **s** ao singular.)

---

1. Complete os espaços com **a** ou **an**:

___ university   ___ hour

___ egg   ___ house   ___ used book   ___ tree

___ car   ___ honour

___ uniform   ___ dog

___ artist   ___ ant

Observações:

- Escreva **a** sempre que o **u** inicial for pronunciado **iu**.
- A maioria das palavras iniciadas por **h**, em inglês, possui **h** aspirado.

honest man   elephant

important date   airplane

excellent book   bus

2. Complete as frases utilizando as expressões do quadro precedidas dos artigos **a** ou **an**:

> Famous Brazilian pilot
> English writer
> American singer
> Brazilian black leader
> Tennis player
> Football player
> Italian artist
> Movie star

a) William Shakespeare was

b) Guga is

c) Julia Roberts is

d) Elvis Presley was

e) Michelangelo was

f) Neymar is

g) Zumbi was

h) Ayrton Senna was

3. Marque a alternativa correta.

She is
( ) a dentist   ( ) an engineer
( ) a teacher   ( ) an artist

4. Marque a alternativa correta.

a) Lilian is
( ) a beaultiful girl
( ) an old woman

b) Complete com **an** ou **a**:
She is not _____ old woman.
She is _____ happy girl.

5. Complete o texto com artigos definidos ou indefinidos e responda a pergunta.

Table
Frog
Lion

I have four legs and ____ tail. I am ____ king of ____ animals.
You can see me in ____ zoo or in ____ forests in Africa.
I can roar. What am I?
You are ____

6. Copie as frases embaixo das fotografias correspondentes.

This is a hat.
This is a happy girl.
This is a husband and his wife.
This is a hot dog.

7. Traduza para inglês.

a) O menino.
b) Os meninos.
c) A menina.
d) As meninas.

8. Siga o modelo.

Rose: **this is a rose**.

a) Tree:
b) Car:
c) Plane:
d) Boy:
e) Girl:
f) Pen:

9. Siga o modelo.

Orange: **that is an orange.**

a) Apple:

b) Egg:

c) Ice cream:

d) Elephant:

e) Umbrella:

f) American boy:

10. Complete com **a** ou **an**.

a) That is ____ American girl.

b) This is ____ English boy.

c) This is ____ egg.

d) That is ____ house.

e) This is ____ table.

f) That is ____ elephant.

g) This is ____ orange.

h) That is ____ pen.

i) That is ____ desk.

Dictation

11. Ouça com atenção o ditado que o professor vai apresentar e escreva.

Review – Lessons 1, 2 and 3

1. Connect (ligue):

day	ano
week	dia
month	baixo
eyes	mês
year	semana
short	alto
tall	cabelo
hair	olhos

2. Escreva, em inglês, os nomes de 6 países onde se fala inglês.

3. Traduza para o inglês.

a) Bom dia.

b) Tchau, até logo.

c) Meu nome é Rose.

ANOTAÇÕES

Lesson 4 – Verb to be: verbo ser ou estar

I'm a little girl, too.
And I have two little dogs.
They're white and brown.

I'm a little girl.
And I have a little rabbit.
It's white.

It is a bird.
It é um pronome neutro, usado para coisas, animais e plantas.

PRESENT TENSE (TEMPO PRESENTE)	SHORT FORM (FORMA ABREVIADA)
I am (eu sou, eu estou)	I'm
You are (você é, você está)	You're
He is (ele é, ele está)	He's
She is (ela é, ela está)	She's
It is (ele, ela é; ele, ela está)	It's
We are (nós somos, nós estamos)	We're
You are (vocês são, vocês estão)	You're
They are (eles, elas são; eles, elas estão)	They're

1. Complete as frases com o verbo **to be**, de acordo com a tradução.

a) _____ a teacher.
(Eu sou uma professora.)

b) _____ engineers.
(Nós somos engenheiros.)

c) _____ a fireman.
(Ele é um bombeiro.)

d) _____ a cook.
(Ele é um cozinheiro.)

e) _____ a waiter.
(Você é um garçom.)

f) _____ singers.
(Vocês são cantores.)

g) _____ basketball players.
(Eles são jogadores de basquete.)

2. Complete com os pronomes **I, we, he, she, it**.

a) _____ is a tree.

b) _____ are students.

c) _____ is a good girl.

d) _____ is a good boy.

e) _____ am a teacher.

3. Siga o modelo e escreva no plural.

I am well.
We are well.

a) I am fine.

b) I am happy.

c) I am an artist.

d) He is a teacher.

e) It is an apple.

f) She is a good singer.

g) You are my friend.

h) She is a hungry.

i) The rose is beautiful.

j) It is red.

k) He is at school.

4. Complete as frases com o verbo **to be** no presente simples.

a) I ____ well.

b) They ____ at school.

c) One and one ____ two.

d) One from eight ____ seven.

e) In spring it ____ warm.

f) In winter it ____ cold.

g) December, January and February ____ winter months in the US.

h) The gifts ____ under the Christmas tree.

i) You ____ my best friend.

j) We ____ at the supermarket now.

k) How ____ you?

l) What ____ your name?

m) She ____ American.

n) What day ____ today? Today ____ Monday.

o) What color ____ your eyes?

p) What color ____ your hair?

q) Your parents ____ young.

5. Traduza para inglês.

a) Você é bonita.

b) Eles são cantores.

c) Vocês estão felizes.

d) Você está feliz.

e) Eu estou pronto.

f) Nós estamos atrasados.

g) Ela é jovem.

6. Siga o modelo.

The girl / beautiful or ugly

Is the girl beautiful or ugly?
The girl is beautiful.
She is beautiful.

The car / dirty or clean

a)

BANCO DE PALAVRAS
você, vocês: you   **é, está:** is
cantor: singer   **feliz:** happy
bonita: beautiful   **atrasado:** late
sou, estou: am   **pronto:** ready
são, estão: are   **velho:** old

The boy / funny or serious

b) _____

The girls fat or thin

c) _____

The man / young or old

d) _____

7. Escreva o verbo **to be** na forma por extenso e abreviada.

Use:	
Am	'm
Is	's
Are	're

I am	I'm
You	you
He	he
She	she
It	it
We	we
You	you
They	they

8. Complete a carta da Sandy com o verbo **to be** no presente simples.

Dear Fred,

My name _____ Sandy.

I _____ very happy to write to you.

I _____ a student at Kennedy High School.

I _____ fourteen years old and my sister Helen _____ ten.

Boris _____ my best friend.
We _____ good students.
We _____ at the same class.

_____ you a good student, too?
Best wishes from
Sandy

9. Complete as lacunas com pronomes pessoais.

a) How old is Sandy?
_____ is fourteen years old.

b) How old is Sandy's sister?
_____ is ten years old.

c) Boris and Sandy are students.
_____ study at Kennedy School.
_____ are in the same class.

10. Escreva as perguntas do quadro de acordo com as respostas.

> What's your address?
> What's your telephone number?
> What's your name?
> How old are you?

a) _____
My name is John.

b) _____
I am ten years old.

c) _____
My telephone number is 5265-4747.

d) _____
I live at 65 California Street.

11. Siga o modelo e monte as frases. Pontue sem esquecer as iniciais maiúsculas.

– hiiamjessica.
– **Hi, I am Jessica.**

a) – nicetomeetyoujessica.

b) – whatisyourname.

c) – mynameisjohn.

d) – howareyoujohn?

e) – iamwellandyou?

f) – iamfinethanksandyou?

g) – iamfinetoo.

12. Complete as lacunas da carta empregando o verbo **to be** no presente simples:

Dear penfriend Silvia,

My first name _____ Cesar and my family name _____ Stein. I _____ from Liverpool (the city of The Beatles) in the north of England.

I _____ eleven years old and I study at Springfield School. I _____ in the seventh grade.

There are twenty-five students in my classroom: eleven girls and fourteen boys.

My favorite sport _____ volleyball and my favorite subject _____ school _____ History.

Here _____ my photo.

Best Wishes,
Cesar

13. Consulte a carta e responda.

First name: **Cesar**

Family name:

City of The Beatles:

Country of The Beatles:

Cesar's age:

Name of the school:

Grade:

Girls in Cesar's classroom:

Boys in Cesar's classroom:

Cesar's favorite sport:

Cesar's favorite subject:

Dictation

14. Ouça com atenção o ditado que o professor vai apresentar e escreva.

Lesson 5 – Is she a teacher?

VERB TO BE (SER, ESTAR) PRESENTE SIMPLES
FORMA INTERROGATIVA E NEGATIVA

VERB TO BE — Verbo SER / Verbo ESTAR

Interrogative form:
Am I ...?
Are you ...?
Is he ...?
Is she ...?
Is it ...?
Are we ...?
Are you ...?
Are they ...?

Negative form:
I am not ...
You are not ...
He is not ...
She is not ...
It is not ...
We are not ...
You are not ...
They are not ...

- **Is she** a teacher?
- No, **she is not**. She is a student.

1. Relacione os adjetivos:

(a) tall   ( ) alta(o)
(b) small, short   ( ) cara(o)
(c) beautiful   ( ) pequena(o)
(d) expensive   ( ) bonita(o)
(e) young   ( ) barata(o)
(f) ugly   ( ) idosa(o)
(g) cheap   ( ) jovem
(h) elderly   ( ) feia(o)
(i) sad   ( ) alegre
(j) joyful   ( ) gentil
(k) kind   ( ) doente
(l) sick   ( ) triste
(m) rude   ( ) nova(o)
(n) new   ( ) rude

2. Siga o modelo:

Mary – tall – short
Is Mary tall?
No, she is not tall.
She is short.

a) Helen – young – elderly

b) the car – old – new

c) the boys – sad – joyful

d) John – rude – kind

e) Monica – well – sick

f) this book – expensive – cheap

3. Escreva as frases na forma negativa.

You are my friend.
You are not my friend.

a) The car is expensive.

b) The teacher is young.

c) Paul is short.

d) Monica is well today.

e) My house is beautiful.

f) Your girlfriend is beautiful.

g) They are old.

4. Complete as frases com o verbo **to be** no presente simples.

a) You ____ a dentist.

b) They ____ teachers.

c) I ____ a taxi driver.

d) Canada ____ a big country.

e) We ____ Brazilians.

O verbo **to be** nas frases acima tem o sentido de:

( ) ser ou ( ) estar?

f) My mother ___ at home.

g) The teachers ___ at school.

h) I ___ in the office.

i) My friends ___ at the beach.

Nos exemplos de f a i, o verbo **to be** tem o sentido de:

( ) ser   ou   ( ) estar?

5. Complete as frases com as formas negativas abreviadas:

'm not, aren't, isn't

a) I ___ not ten, I ___ eleven.

b) I ___ not from Portugal, I ___ from Brazil.

c) Robert and Joseph ___ doctors, they are dentists.

d) Carol ___ well, she's sick.

e) You ___ at school, you are at home.

f) Porto Alegre ___ in the north of Brazil, it is in the south.

6. Siga o modelo e substitua os nomes por pronomes com o verbo **to be** na forma abreviada:

(Brazil) – a big country.
It's a big country.

a) (The horse and the cow) – domestic animals.

b) (Roberto Carlos) – a great singer.

c) (Mary and I) – in the club.

d) (The pen and the pencil) – on the table.

e) (The Amazon forest) – marvelous.

7. Siga o modelo.

You are ugly. (beautiful)
You aren't ugly. You are beautiful.

a) Your car is old. (new)

c) The sunflower is green. (yellow)

d) Henry is sad. (joyful)

e) They are in the park. (at home)

8. Relacione as frases da coluna A com as da coluna B:

Coluna A

– Hi!

– What's your name?

– How old are you?

– Where are you from?

– See you later.

Coluna B

– I am 11 years old.

– Hello.

– Goodbye!

– My name is Monica.

– I am from Brasilia.

9. Complete o exercício, usando as formas abreviadas: 'm not, isn't, aren't, 'm 's, 're.

I'm not John. I'm Robert.

a) I _____ well. _____ sick.

b) She _____ American. She _____ Brazilian.

c) You _____ not tall. You _____ short.

d) It _____ late. It _____ early.

e) It _____ Saturday. It _____ Sunday.

10. Pinte as áreas com pontos.

a) What's hidden in the picture?

Are they things?   Yes ( ) No ( )
Are they animals? Yes ( ) No ( )
Are they people?   Yes ( ) No ( )

b) What are they?

They _____

Lesson 6 – Introducing people

Sam: This is my family. This is my wife Grace.
Jack: Nice to meet you, Grace.
Grace: Nice to meet you, too.
Sam: And these are my children Kenny and Mike.
Jack: Hi!
Mike and Kenny: Hi!

DEMONSTRATIVES:
Singular
this (este, esta, isto)

Plural
these (estes, estas)

1. Aprenda a apresentar pessoas, em inglês, encenando o texto anterior com um colega. Modifique os nomes e a relação que você tem com as pessoas:

WORD BANK	
father: pai	**son:** filho
mother: mãe	**daughter:** filha
wife: esposa	**parents:** pais
husband: marido	**children:** filhos
brother: irmão	**friend:** amigo
sister: irmã	**classmate:** colega de classe

2. O título "**Introducing people**" significa:
   ( ) apresentando ao povo
   ( ) apresentando pessoas
   ( ) introduzindo ao povo

3. Quem está apresentando a família ao Jack?

4. Quem o Sam apresenta primeiro ao Jack?

5. Como Jack responde à apresentação à Grace?

6. Com que palavra Jack cumprimenta os filhos de Sam?
( ) Hello!   ( ) Hi!   ( ) Goodbye

7. A palavra "children", no texto, significa:
( ) crianças
( ) criança
( ) filhos

8. Como se chamam os filhos (children) de Sam e Grace?

9. Nos quadros abaixo, recorte e cole figuras de homem, mulher, menino e menina e escreva em inglês as palavras que estão entre parênteses.

(pais)

(esposo)

(esposa)

(filho)

(filha)

(filhos)

(irmão)

(irmã)

10. Complete a cruzada, traduzindo as palavras do português para o inglês:

1 - filha
2 - filho
3 - filhos
4 - irmã
5 - irmão
6 - pais
7 - marido
8 - esposa

11. Relacione as frases de acordo com o sentido.

This is my son.   Estes são meus pais.

This is my daughter   Este é meu filho.

These are my children   Estes são meus filhos.

These are my parents.   Esta é minha filha.

12. Escreva no plural.

a) This is my sister.
   These

b) This is my brother.
   These

c) This is my daughter.

d) This is my little son and daughter.

Dictation

13. Ouça com atenção o ditado que o professor vai apresentar e escreva.

ANOTAÇÕES

Review – Lessons 4, 5 and 6

1. Siga os pontos (Follow the dots).

What's this?

It's ( ) a dog   ( ) a bird

( ) a boy   ( ) an orange

2. Responda:

a) Who are you? (Robert)

b) How are you? (well)

c) What's your occupation? (student)

3. Complete com **a** ou **an**:

a) I am _____ teacher.

b) You are _____ artist.

c) I am _____ student.

d) You are _____ office-boy.

e) Are you _____ secretary?

f) I am _____ English player.

g) I am _____ American pilot.

h) You are _____ Italian teacher.

4. Complete com: **how, nice, am, name**:

a) _____ are you?

b) I _____ a singer.

c) What's your _____ ?

d) _____ to meet you!

5. Relacione os opostos.

- rude • • expensive
- young • • short
- ugly • • kind
- well • • old
- dirty • • beautiful
- cheap • • sick
- joyful • • clean
- tall • • sad

6. Escreva as frases no plural.
(Obs.: o artigo **a(an)** não é usado no plural. Os adjetivos ficam invariáveis.)

a) I am a good student.

b) She is a beautiful girl.

c) It is an expensive car.

d) You are my friend.

7. Escreva as frases na forma interrogativa.

a) She is sad.

b) They are good boys.

c) You are well.

d) Your hands are dirty.

8. Escreva as frases na forma negativa.

a) You are my friend.

b) They are singers.

c) Your girlfriend is joyful.

d) We are sick.

9. Complete as frases usando **my** e **your**.

a) I am Paul and you are Alice.

_____ name is Paul and _____ name is Alice.

b) You are Freddy and I am Rose.

_____ name is Freddy and _____ name is Rose.

10. Substitua os nomes pelos pronomes **they, he, she, it**:

a) Alan is a good student.
_____ is a good student.

b) The lion is an animal.
_____ is an animal.

c) My friends are nice.
_____ are nice.

d) The sun is a star.
_____ is a star.

e) Rose is my sister.
_____ is my sister.

f) Puppy is my dog.
_____ is my dog.

g) The parrots are funny.
_____ are funny.

h) Djavan is a singer
_____ is a singer.

ANOTAÇÕES

Lesson 7 – Demonstratives

*Dad! Dad! Look at **that** big fish!*

***That** is not a fish. It's a whale.*

SINGULAR	PLURAL
This (este, esta, isto)	**These** (estes, estas)
That (aquele, aquela, aquilo)	**Those** (aqueles, aquelas)

This e **these** são usados para indicar seres e objetos que estão perto da pessoa que fala; **that** e **those**, para indicar seres e objetos distantes da pessoa que fala.

1. Observe os modelos. Faça perguntas empregando **this** ou **that** de acordo com as figuras. A seguir responda afirmativamente.

What is this?
This is a book.

What is that?
That is an airplane.

a)

b)

c)

d)

e)

2. Siga o modelo e escreva as frases no singular e no plural:

an egg   eggs

This is an egg.   These are eggs.

a) a car   cars

b) a house   houses

3. Siga o modelo. Use **this**, **that**, **these**, **those**.

This is a car, but that is a bus.

(car – bus)

a) (birds – airplanes)

b) (book – magazine)

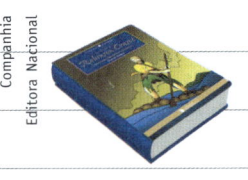

4. Ordene as palavras abaixo e monte uma frase.

Dad, / that / of / name / what / the / is / fruit?

5. Escreva as frases no plural. Observe que os adjetivos em inglês ficam invariáveis.

> This car is very expensive.
> **These cars are very expensive.**

a) This cake is delicious.

b) That ship is far from the port.

c) That boy is my friend.

6. Faça perguntas, em inglês, apontando para:

a) uma coisa perto de você;
   What is this?

b) uma pessoa longe de você;

c) várias coisas perto de você;

d) várias pessoas longe de você;

7. Traduza para o português.
   – What is that in the sky?
   – It is a red kite.

8. Traduza para o inglês:
   – O que é isto?
   – Isto é uma laranja.

9. Observe as figuras na cruzadinha e responda às perguntas.

1. What is that?

2. What is this?

3. What are those?

4. What is that?

5. What is this?

6. What are these?

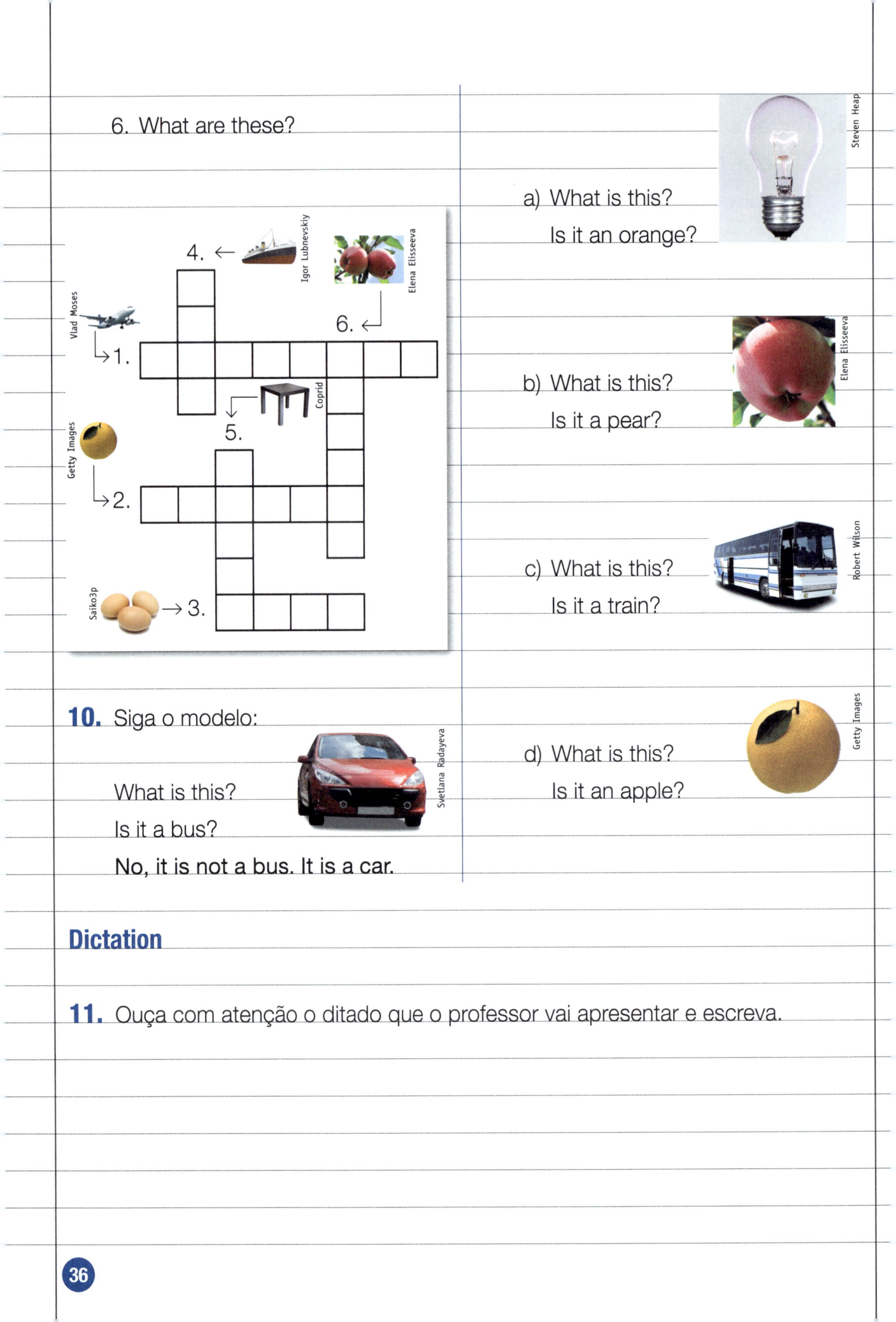

a) What is this?
Is it an orange?

b) What is this?
Is it a pear?

c) What is this?
Is it a train?

10. Siga o modelo:

What is this?
Is it a bus?
No, it is not a bus. It is a car.

d) What is this?
Is it an apple?

Dictation

11. Ouça com atenção o ditado que o professor vai apresentar e escreva.

Lesson 8 – Meeting people – I

- Good morning.
- Good morning.
- How are you?
- I am well, thanks.
- What is your name?
- My name is Robert.
- What is your occupation?
- I am a teacher.

INTERROGATIVE WORDS

How: como
How are you?
Como vai você?

What: qual, quais, o que
What is your name?
Qual é seu nome?

Who: quem
Who is that man?
Quem é aquele homem?

Where: onde
Where is your friend?
Onde está seu amigo?

---

1. Reescreva as perguntas de acordo com as respostas.

> How old are you?
> What is your name?
> What is your telephone number?
> What is your address?
> What is your occupation?

a) _____
   My name is Jennifer.

b) _____
   I'm eleven.

c) _____
   I live at 25 Paris Street.

d) _____
   8888-7777

e) _____
   I am a dentist.

2. Complete as perguntas e dê respostas relativas a você mesmo.

a) What _____ your first name?
   My first name is

b) What _____ your surname?
My surname is _____

c) When _____ your birthday?
My birthday is _____

d) Where _____ from?
I am from _____

e) What _____ telephone number?
My telephone number is _____

f) What _____ address?
I live at _____

g) What color _____ hair?
My hair is _____

h) What color _____ eyes?
My eyes are _____

3. Observe o modelo, leia as respostas e faça as perguntas.

a) **What is your favorite sport?**
My favorite sport is swimming.

b) _____
My favorite sport is football.

c) _____
My favorite movie star is Julia Roberts.

d) _____
My favorite hobby is listening to music.

e) _____
My favorite color is blue.

f) _____
My favorite food is rice and beans.

4. Arranje as palavras do quadro e monte o diálogo.

> Hi!
> Hi!
> What'syourname?
> MynameisLucy.
> HowareyouLucy?
> Iamfinethanksandyou?
> Howoldareyou?
> Iamelevenyearsold.
> Whereareyoufrom?
> IamfromEngland.

Cuidado com a pontuação e o emprego de letras maiúsculas.

The rooms of the house

The rooms of the house are: hall, living room, dining room, bedroom, bathroom, study area, kitchen and garage.

I sleep in the bedroom, take a shower in the bathroom, cook in the kitchen, eat in the dining room, do my homework in the study area and watch TV in the living room.

Meals
Breakfast is at seven in the morning.
Lunch is at one in the afternoon.
Tea is at five in the afternoon.
Dinner is at eight in the evening.

6. Responda às perguntas sobre o texto acima.

a) What are the rooms of the house?

5. Responda às perguntas sobre o texto acima.

a) When is breakfast time?

b) Where do you sleep?

b) When is lunch time?

c) Where do you take a shower?

c) When is tea time?

d) Where do you cook?

d) When is dinner time?

e) Where do you eat?

e) What are the meals of the day?

f) Where do you do your homework?

g) Where do you watch TV?

h) Where do you park your car?
   ( ) in the hall.
   ( ) in the bathroom.
   ( ) in the garage.

7. Traduza a carta abaixo:

Dear Meg,
   This letter is to tell you that we are very happy to receive you in our home.
   Our house has two floors.
   Upstairs there are three bedrooms and two bathrooms. There is also a small study area with a TV set and a computer.
   Downstairs there are a living room, a dining room, a kitchen and a toilet.
   Our house has a garage and a little garden, too.
   In the garage there are two bikes, a car, some toys and garden tools.
   Our house is not modern, but you are welcome here.
   Write soon, please, and tell us the day of your arrival.
   Love from,
   Grace

8. Siga o modelo e responda, usando as expressões entre parênteses.
   Where is New York?
   (in the United States)
   New York is in the United States.

a) Where is Paris? (in France)

b) Where is Berlin? (in Germany)

c) Where is London? (in England)

d) Where is Rome? (in Italy)

e) Where is Tokyo? (in Japan)

f) Where do you live? (in Rio)

g) Where do you live?
   (in Florianópolis)

h) Where do you live? (in Recife)

i) Where do you live?
   (on Alvorada Street)

j) Where do you live?
   (on Republica Avenue)

k) Where do you live?
   (at 7 Rui Barbosa Street)

l) Where do you live?
   (at 45 Palmeiras Square)

9. Faça perguntas de acordo com as respostas, siga o modelo.

When do you get up?
(Quando você se levanta?)
I get up at 7 o'clock.
(Eu me levanto às 7 horas.)

a)
I go to school at 7:30 a.m.
(a.m. [ante meridiem]: antes do meio-dia)

b)
I come from school at midday.

c)
I have lunch at one o'clock.

d)
I practice sports in the afternoon.

e)
I watch TV in the evening.

f) _____
My birthday is on the first of May.

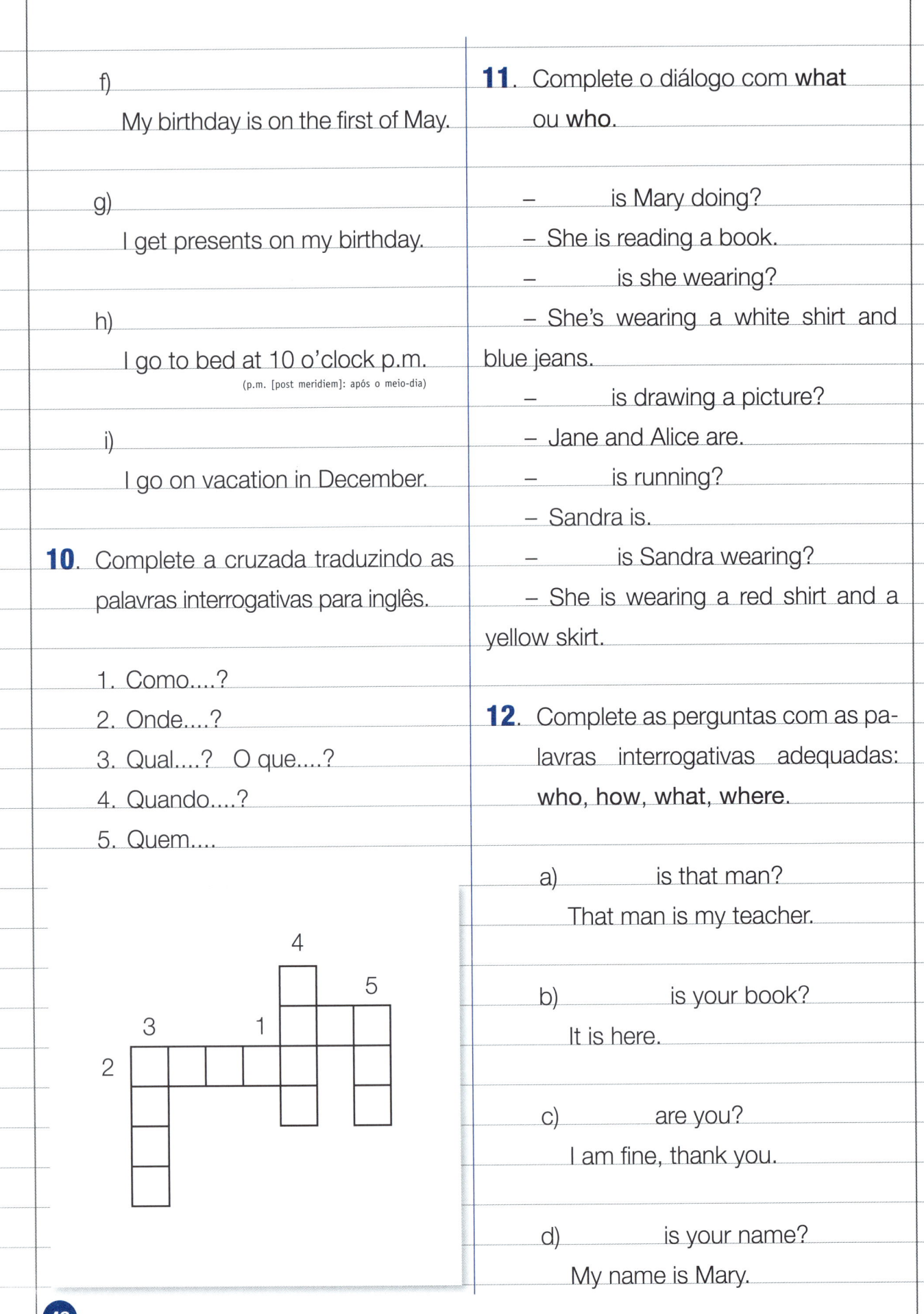

g) _____
I get presents on my birthday.

h) _____
I go to bed at 10 o'clock p.m.
(p.m. [post meridiem]: após o meio-dia)

i) _____
I go on vacation in December.

10. Complete a cruzada traduzindo as palavras interrogativas para inglês.

1. Como....?
2. Onde....?
3. Qual....? O que....?
4. Quando....?
5. Quem....

11. Complete o diálogo com **what** ou **who**.

– _____ is Mary doing?
– She is reading a book.
– _____ is she wearing?
– She's wearing a white shirt and blue jeans.
– _____ is drawing a picture?
– Jane and Alice are.
– _____ is running?
– Sandra is.
– _____ is Sandra wearing?
– She is wearing a red shirt and a yellow skirt.

12. Complete as perguntas com as palavras interrogativas adequadas: **who, how, what, where.**

a) _____ is that man?
That man is my teacher.

b) _____ is your book?
It is here.

c) _____ are you?
I am fine, thank you.

d) _____ is your name?
My name is Mary.

e) _____ has a neck, but has no head?
It's a bootle.

13. Siga o modelo:
Nancy / secretary
Who are you?
I am Nancy. I am a secretary.

a) Donald / farmer

b) Julie / reporter

c) Betty / student

Lesson 9 – Meeting people – II

– **What** is your name?
– My name is Janet.

– **How** are you, Janet?
– I am well, thank you.

– **When** is your birthday?
– My birthday is in January.

– **Where** are you from?
– I am from California.

INTERROGATIVE WORDS

What: qual, o que.   **How:** como.   **When:** quando.   **Where:** onde.

MONTHS

January – February – March – April – May – June
July – August – September – October – November – December

Obs.: Os nomes dos meses, em inglês, são iniciados com letra maiúscula.

1. Observe o modelo, faça a pergunta e dê a resposta.

John – January
– When is your birthday, John?
– My birthday is in January.

a) Mary – February

b) Selma – March

2. Observe o modelo e responda às perguntas.
– Where are you from? (Rio)
– I am from Rio.

a) – Where is she from?
   (Fortaleza)

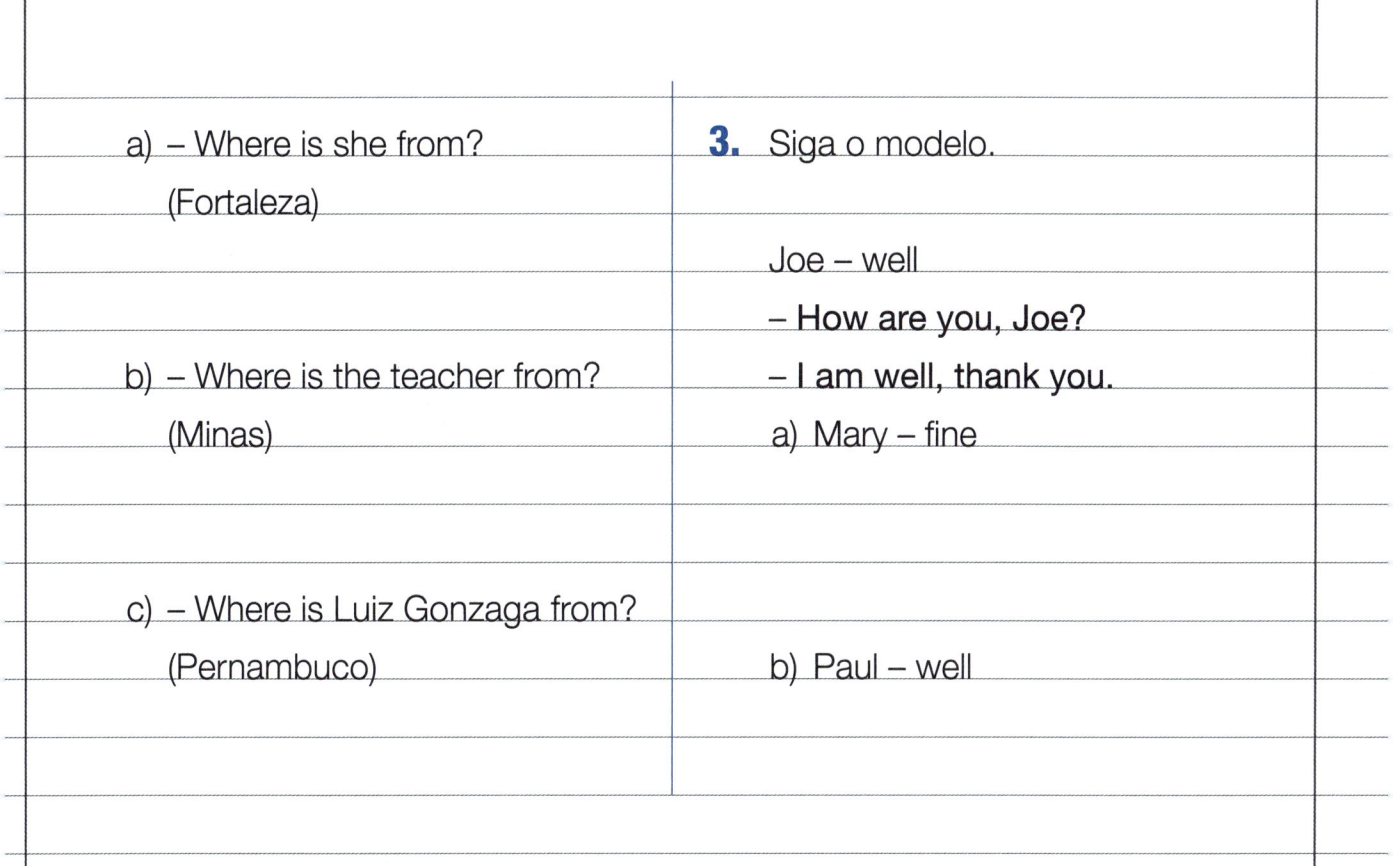

b) – Where is the teacher from?
   (Minas)

c) – Where is Luiz Gonzaga from?
   (Pernambuco)

3. Siga o modelo.

   Joe – well
   – How are you, Joe?
   – I am well, thank you.
   a) Mary – fine

   b) Paul – well

4. Complete a cruzadinha, traduzindo os meses do ano:

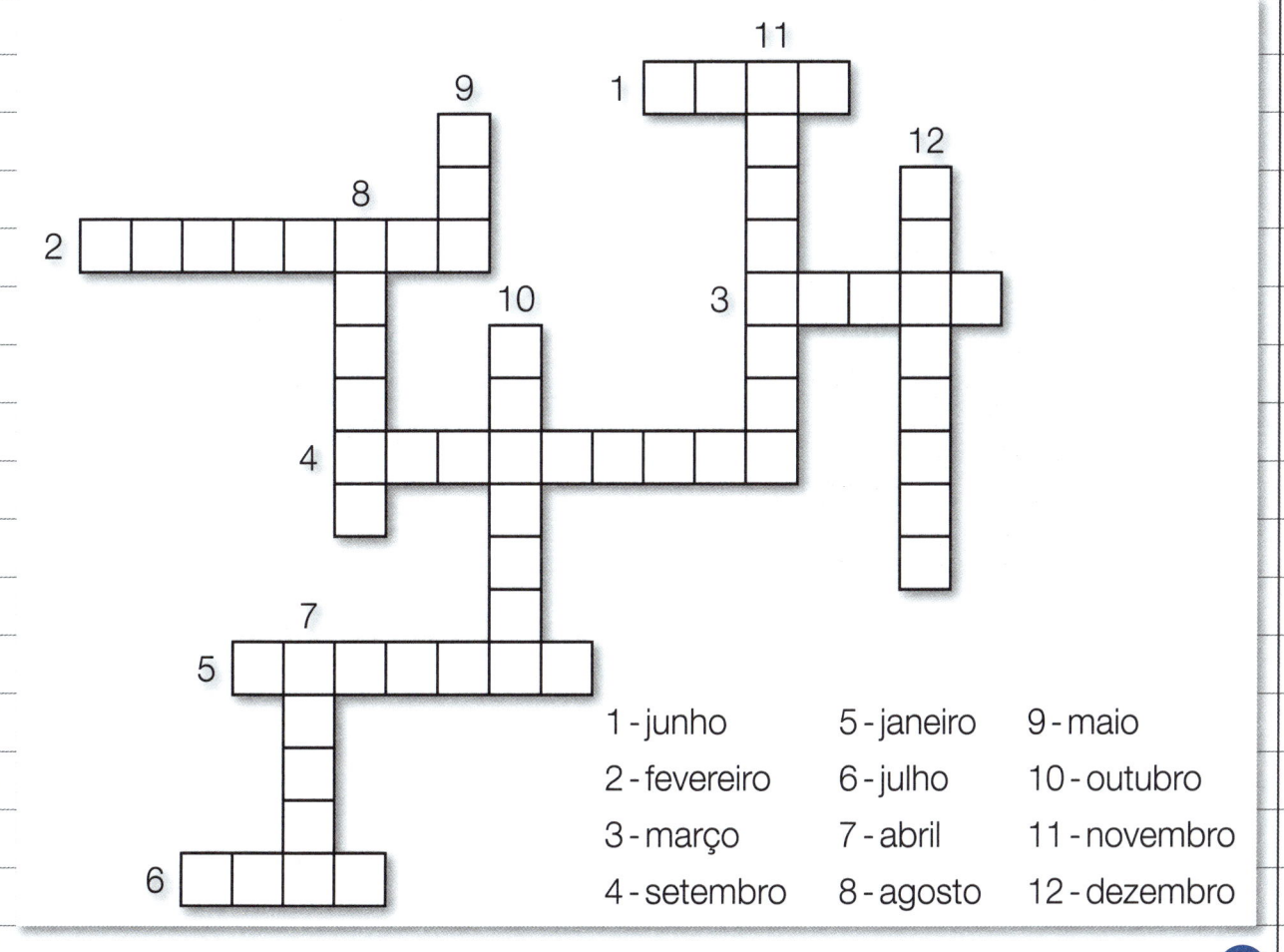

1 - junho   5 - janeiro   9 - maio
2 - fevereiro   6 - julho   10 - outubro
3 - março   7 - abril   11 - novembro
4 - setembro   8 - agosto   12 - dezembro

5. Observe as figuras e responda.

a) Who is the writer in the picture? Is he Machado de Assis or William Shakespeare?

The writer in

b) Who is the woman in the picture? Is she Virginia Wolf or Mona Lisa?

The woman in

c) Who is the scientist in the picture?

d) Who is the politician in the picture?

e) Who is the football player in the picture?

Dictation

6. Ouça com atenção o ditado que o professor vai apresentar e escreva.

ANOTAÇÕES

Lesson 10 – Where are you from?

– Where are you from?
– I am from Brazil. I am Brazilian. I am going to Italy. And you? Where are you from?
– I'm from Japan. I am Japanese.

NATIONALITY ADJECTIVES (adjetivos pátrios)

Os adjetivos pátrios se escrevem sempre com inicial maiúscula: **American, African, Brazilian, French, English, Italian, Spanish, German, Japanese, Chinese, Portuguese...**

O adjetivo, em inglês, permanece invariável e vem antes do substantivo:
American girl – **American** girls
American boy – **American** boys
beautiful girl – **beautiful** girls
beautiful bird – **beautiful** birds

Os adjetivos pátrios, quando substantivados, variam no plural, mas permanecem invariáveis os terminados em **s**, **se**, **sh**, **ch**, como **Swiss, Japanese, Chinese, English, French.**

Observe:
Brazilians like football.
They are **Japanese**.

from → to

- A preposição **from** indica origem.
- A preposição **to** indica destino.

I come **from** Brazil and I am going **to** France.
(Eu venho do Brasil e estou indo para a França.)

1. Traduza o diálogo de introdução.

2. Observe os modelos e responda:
Are you Brazilian? (Brazil)
Yes, I am Brazilian. I am from Brazil.

a) Are you Mexican? (Mexico)

b) Are you German? (Germany)

c) Are you Japanese? (Japan)

Are you Brazilian? (English)
No, I am not Brazilian.
I am English.

d) Are you English? (Mexican)

e) Are you Mexican? (German)

f) Are you German? (Japanese)

American / French
Is he American?
No, he is not American.
He is French.

g) Mexican / Brazilian

h) Italian / Portuguese

Mexico / Brazil
Is she from Mexico?
No, she is not from Mexico.
She is from Brazil.

i) America / France

He / Japan
Where is he from?
He is from Japan.

j) She / England

k) He / Italy

3. Preencha a cruzadinha com os adjetivos pátrios.

1. Estados Unidos
2. França
3. Itália
4. Japão
5. Inglaterra
6. China
7. Brasil
8. Alemanha
9. Portugal
10. Suíça

4. Observe os produtos, faça perguntas e responda conforme o modelo.

Where is this cheese from?
This cheese is from Switzerland.
It is a Swiss cheese.

Cheese

a)

It is a Swiss watch.

Watch

b)

This car is from Germany.

Car

c)

It is a Japanese TV set.

TV

IMPORTAÇÃO E EXPORTAÇÃO

O Brasil vem se destacando pelo vigor de suas exportações de soja, algodão, milho, suco de laranja, café, aço, carros etc., mas importa máquinas, relógios, remédios, computadores, carros etc. Esses produtos têm sua origem identificada pela expressão **Made in** (**Japan, Germany...**) ou com a preposição **from** (**Brazil, China...**).

Made in: fabricado em..., feito em...
From: proveniente de...
 (origem do produto).
Imported from: (importado de)
Exported to: (exportado para)

50

d)
This toy is from China.

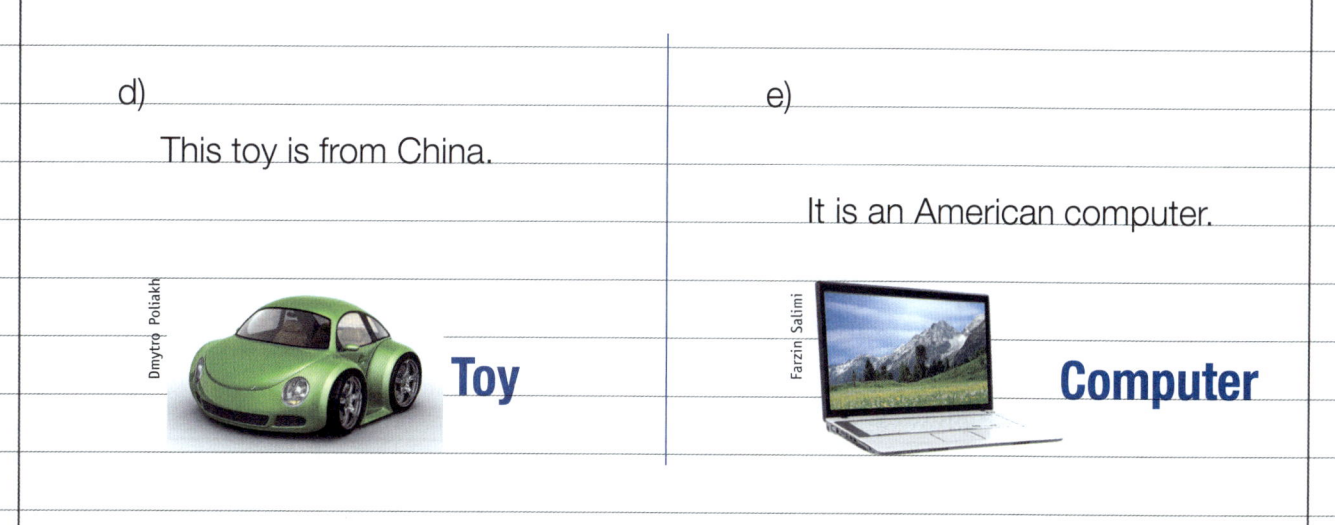

Toy

e)
It is an American computer.

Computer

5. Uma turista italiana está sendo entrevista por um repórter. Ela veio ver a Copa do Mundo. Traduza o diálogo para português.

Reporter: Welcome to Brazil, the country of football! Where are you from?
Tourist: Thank you very much! I'm from Italy.

Reporter: Do you like football?
Tourist: Yes! I like football very much! I want to see the football World Cup in Brazil.

Reporter: It's will be a great happening! Enjoy it!
Tourist: Thank you!

Review – Lessons 7, 8, 9 and 10

1. Word hunt. Find out the nationalities corresponding to these countries: Brazil, England, United States, Japan, Germany, Italy, Mexico, France, Portugal, Spain, China, Egypt, Canada, Australia.

K	P	T	R	D	J	A	P	A	N	E	S	E	T	L
V	T	D	A	L	P	O	R	T	T	R	A	N	C	H
F	R	E	N	C	H	L	O	J	M	N	T	R	S	A
T	Y	U	E	F	G	I	T	A	L	I	A	N	C	V
B	R	A	Z	I	L	I	A	N	N	F	O	O	T	B
B	T	D	L	S	E	N	G	L	I	S	H	Q	N	Y
A	M	E	R	I	C	A	N	C	S	T	L	M	N	S
N	L	S	D	U	C	G	E	R	M	A	N	L	G	D
C	A	N	A	D	I	A	N	B	T	R	S	L	D	F
T	S	D	L	A	U	S	T	R	A	L	I	A	N	S
D	S	T	D	L	U	C	H	I	N	E	S	E	J	G
S	P	A	N	I	S	H	D	L	K	J	H	G	F	R
E	G	Y	P	T	I	A	N	W	Q	Z	X	C	M	R
F	G	H	W	P	O	R	T	U	G	U	E	S	E	X
Q	W	S	M	E	X	I	C	A	N	B	V	C	K	S

2. Siga o modelo e escreva as frases no plural.

That is a nice shop.
Those are nice shops.

a) That is a beautiful bird.

b) That train, that ship and that boat are very old.

c) That magazine is not interesting.

d) That book is new.

e) This is a good teacher.

3. Escreva as frases na forma interrogativa.

a) You are Brazilian.

b) She is German.

c) They are Americans.

d) John and Mark are from England.

4. Traduza para o inglês.

a) De onde você é?

b) Você é da Itália?

c) Você é da China, eles são do Japão e ela é da França.

d) Isto é um livro e aquilo é uma revista.

e) Quem é aquele homem?

f) Onde estão seus amigos?

g) Quando é seu aniversário?

Dictation

5. Ouça com atenção o ditado que o professor vai apresentar e escreva.

Lesson 11 – Imperative – affirmative form

Where is Atlantic Street, please?

Go ahead two blocks and turn right.

IMPERATIVO – FORMA AFIRMATIVA

O imperativo indica uma ordem, um pedido ou um conselho.

Em inglês, formamos o imperativo afirmativo tirando a partícula **to** do infinitivo do verbo.

Observe:

　Infinitivo: **to turn** right (virar à direita)

　Imperativo: **turn** right (Vire à direita)

1. Complete as frases, usando os verbos do quadro no imperativo afirmativo.

to drink – to sharpen – to go
to open – to look – to erase

a) _____ your books.

b) _____ to the blackboard.

c) _____ the blackboard.

d) _____ some water.

e) _____ your pencil.

f) _____ at me.

2. Dê ordens contrárias às apresentadas, usando os verbos do quadro.

> to come back   to unbutton
> to put   to take off
> to turn on   to sit down
> to turn off   to open

a) Close your book.
    _____ your book.

b) Turn on the water.
    _____ the water.

c) Turn off the lights.
    _____ the lights.

d) Go to the blackboard.
    _____ from the blackboard.

e) Raise your hands.
    _____ your hands down.

f) Stand up.

g) Button your shirt.
    _____ your shirt.

h) Put on your coat.
    _____ your coat.

3. Observe o exemplo e forme frases imperativas.
(Obs.: Não se coloca vírgula após a palavra **please**, quando esta aparece em início de frase.)

Please (**to call**) the doctor.
Please call the doctor.

a) Please (**to wait**) a moment.

b) Please (**to open**) the door.

c) Please (**to shut**) the window.

d) Please (**to write**) your name.

e) Please (**to come**) here.

f) Please (**to sit**) down.

4. Traduza para português.

a) Preserve and protect nature.

b) Live and let live.

5. Crie frases no imperativo afirmativo, usando estes verbos:

a) to open:

b) to close:

c) to wait:

d) to look:

e) to pay:

6. Construa frases no imperativo afirmativo, colocando em ordem as palavras dadas.

a) go – blackboard – to – the

b) go – to – place – your

c) books – open – your

d) down – please – sit

e) moment – a – wait

f) me – show – copybook – your

g) page – on – read – seven

h) at – car – look – the

Lesson 12 – Imperative – negative form

IMPERATIVO – FORMA NEGATIVA

Para formar o imperativo negativo em inglês, basta tirar a partícula **to** do infinitivo do verbo e colocar a negativa **don't** em seu lugar. Veja:

To talk (falar, conversar)
↓
Don't talk! (Não fale, não converse)

A palavra **please** significa "por favor" e é usada com o imperativo para indicar gentileza na maneira de dar ordens ou fazer pedidos:

– Sit down, **please**. **Please** sit down.
– Don't sit down, **please**. **Please** don't sit down.

> Don't talk here, please! Silence!

(Observe que a palavra **please** pode vir no começo ou no fim da frase; se vier no fim da frase é precedida por uma vírgula.)

1. Mude as frases do imperativo afirmativo para o imperativo negativo.

a) Wait for me.

b) Stop the car.

c) Drive fast.

d) Open the window.

e) Smoke here.

f) Go away.

g) Cross the street.

h) Go there.

BANCO DE PALAVRAS

abrir: open	**por favor**: please
fechar: close	**seu**: your
porta: door	**aqui**: here
vir: come	**não**: don't

2. Traduza para o inglês.

a) Abra seu livro, por favor.

b) Por favor, não feche a porta.

c) Não fume, por favor.

d) Por favor, venha aqui.

3. Traduza para o português.

– Please tell me the way to Victoria Station.

– That's easy. Go to the end of this street and turn right.

4. Escreva a ordem embaixo do sinal correspondente.

> Don't turn left.   Turn right.
> Don't turn right.   Don't ride bicycles.

Traffic signs

Ligue as frases aos sinais de trânsito.

Pay attention to school zone.

Respect the traffic lights.

Avoid danger: Drive slowly.

Don't horn.

Pay attention to children.

Don't park here.

Pedestrians: Don't go.

Respect the speed limit.

Fasten your seat belt.

Cross on the zebra.

Disabled: Park here.

5. Relacione a coluna A com a coluna B:

Seja eficiente.	Don't be arrogant.
Fique atento.	Don't get angry.
Fique quieto.	Be efficient.
Não fique zangado.	Be quiet.
Não seja arrogante.	Be attentive.

6. Ordene as palavras e forme frases no imperativo.

a) classmates – with – honest – and sincere – be – your

b) people – don't – deceive

c) your – best – do

d) arrive – don't – late

7. Relacione as traduções com o exercício 6.

( ) Faça o melhor.
( ) Não chegue atrasado.
( ) Seja honesto e sincero com seus colegas de classe.
( ) Não engane as pessoas.

8. Relacione as colunas:

Respect each other.	Não faça barulho.
Enjoy yourselves.	Não fale alto.
Don't make noise.	Divirtam-se.
Don't speak loud.	Respeitem-se.

Dictation

9. Ouça com atenção o ditado que o professor vai apresentar e escreva.

A trip in town

Places to go – Imperative

From the bus station to the shopping center.

Use a button or a coin and a 2 dice.

SCORE: PLAYER A – _____   PLAYER B – _____

#	Square
1	(bus station)
2	
3	GO TO THE SKYSCRAPER
4	
17	RETURN TO THE BOOKSHOP
18	
19	RETURN TO THE PARK
20	
21	(soccer stadium)
22	
23	RETURN TO THE SOCCER STADIUM
24	
25	GO TO THE BRIDGE
33	RETURN TO THE HOSPITAL
34	
35	STAY HERE FOR ONE TURN
36	
37	MISS A TURN
38	

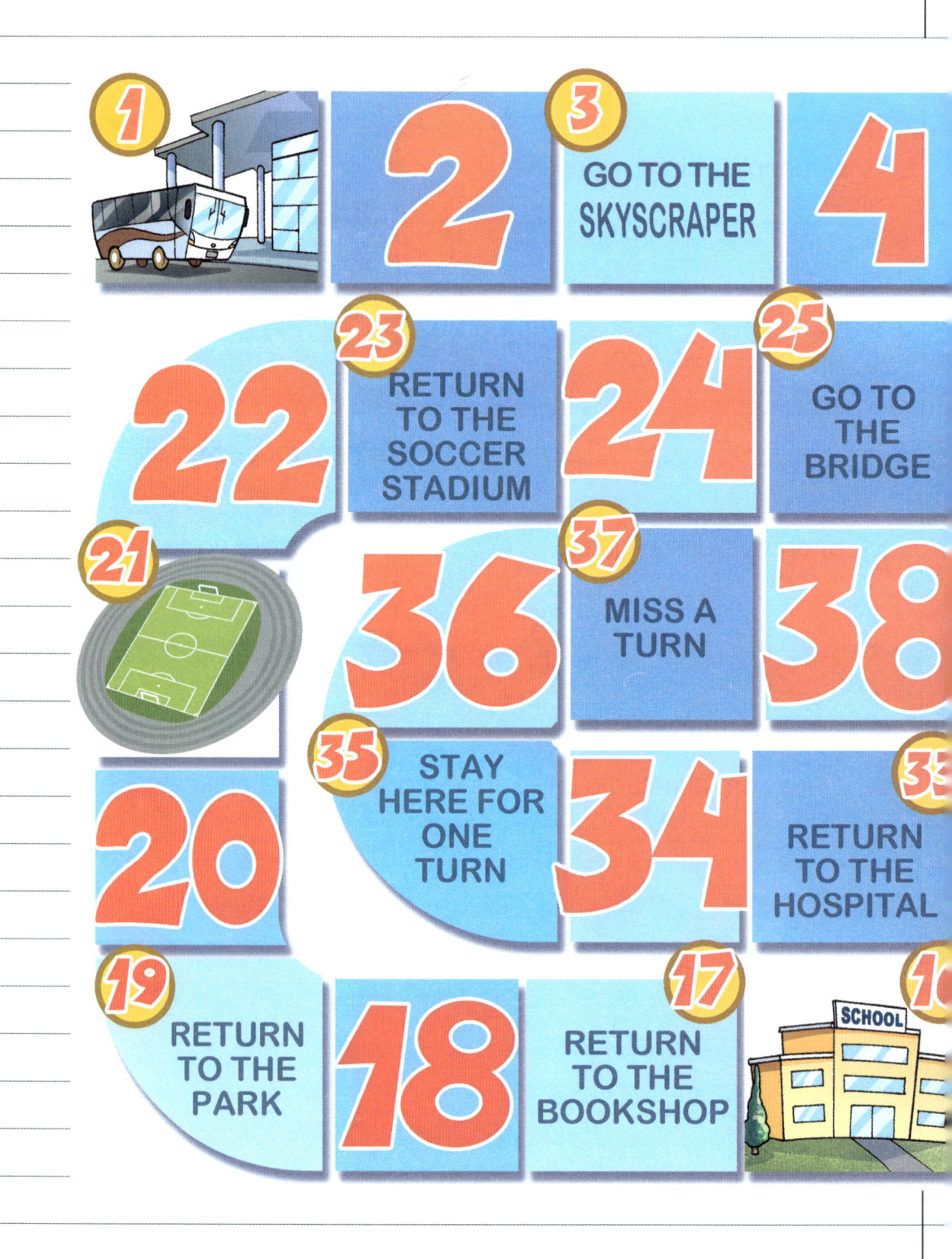

62

WORD BANK

trip: viagem
town: cidade
from: de
places: lugares
go: vá, ir
return: retorne, volte

miss a turn: perde a vez
skyscraper: arranha-céu
church: igreja
stay here: fique aqui
bookshop: livraria
bridge: ponte

score: contagem de pontos
button: botão
coin: moeda
dice: dados
to: para

5 — STOP HERE FOR TWO TURNS
6
7
8
9 — STAY HERE FOR ONE TURN
10
11
12
13 — GO AHEAD TO THE SCHOOL
14
15
26
27
28
29 — MISS A TURN
30
31
32
39 — STOP HERE FOR TWO TURNS
FINISH 40

Lesson 13 – Different bedrooms

This is John's bedroom.
His bedroom is always a mess!

Ana's bedroom is so different!
Her bedroom is clean and tidy.

POSSESSIVES: HIS – HER
His: dele, seu, sua, seus, suas.
Her: dela, seu, sua, seus, suas.

JIM
Look at the boy in the picture.
What color is **his** hair?
His hair is black.
What color is **his** shirt?
His shirt is red.
What color are **his** pants?
His pants are blue.

KATE
Look at the girl in the picture.
What color is **her** hair?
Her hair is blonde.
What color is **her** shirt?
Her shirt is blue.
What color are **her** pants?
Her pants are white.

1. Leia os textos sobre Jim and Jake e responda.

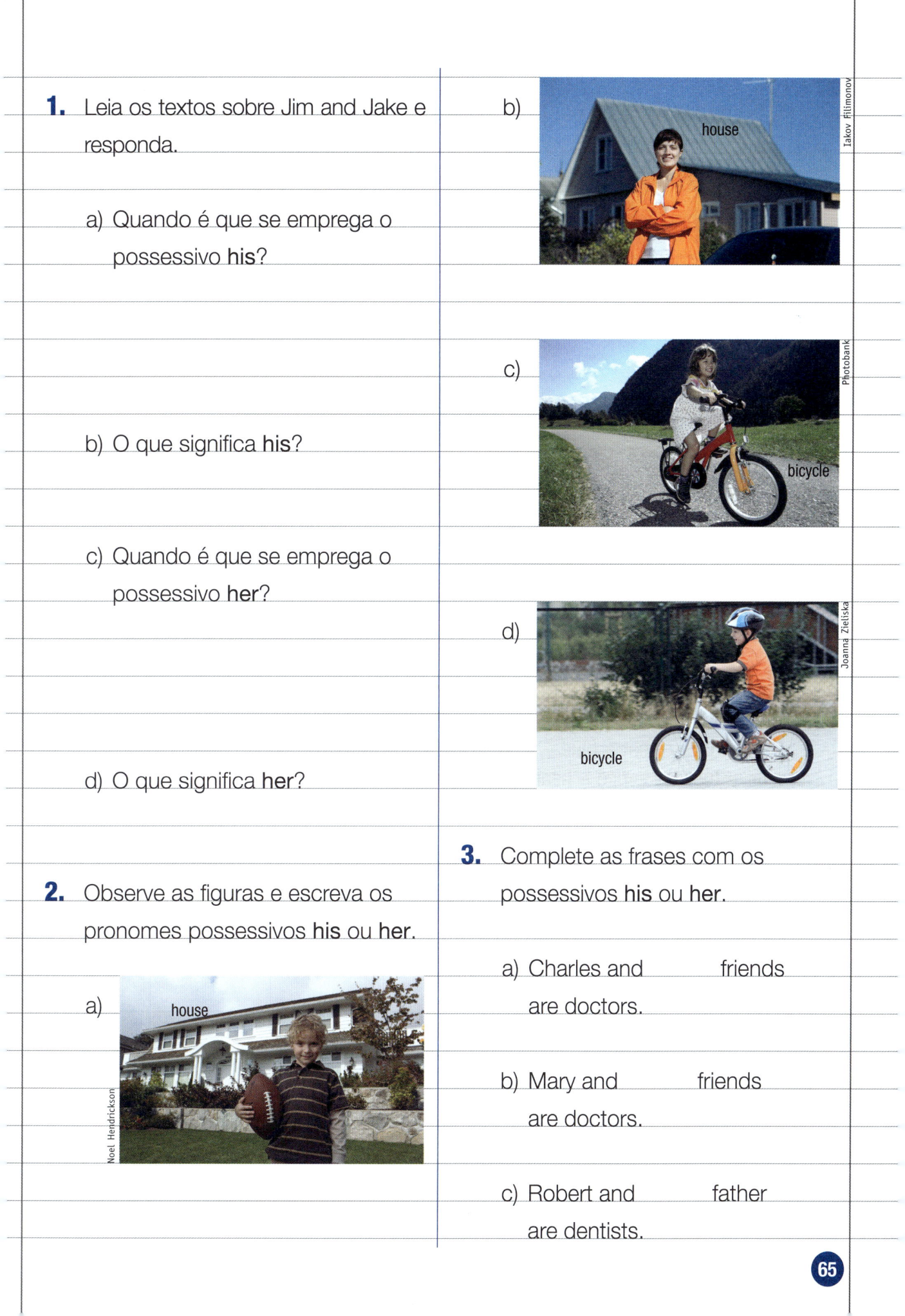

a) Quando é que se emprega o possessivo **his**?

b) O que significa **his**?

c) Quando é que se emprega o possessivo **her**?

d) O que significa **her**?

2. Observe as figuras e escreva os pronomes possessivos **his** ou **her**.

a) [house]

b) [house]

c) [bicycle]

d) [bicycle]

3. Complete as frases com os possessivos **his** ou **her**.

a) Charles and _____ friends are doctors.

b) Mary and _____ friends are doctors.

c) Robert and _____ father are dentists.

d) Karen and _____ sister are students.

e) Susan and _____ brother are teachers.

f) Thomas and _____ friends are pilots.

4. Faça como o modelo:

(house – Jenny)

This house belongs to Jenny. It's her house.

a) (house – Bob)

b) (bike – Liza)

c) (bike – Jeff)

5. Classifique as palavras de acordo com os assuntos; consulte o vocabulário.

apple – bread – yellow – Geography – rabbit – horse – Friday – dog – Sunday
salad – black – English – soda – Saturday – white – water – mango
Monday – meat – blue – Mathematics – sandwich – grey – History – cat
orange – Tuesday – rice – beans – parrot – brown – lion – pear – Wednesday – red
beef – tiger – green – Science – juice – coffee – peach – cheese

Fruit	Days of the week	Colors	Food	Animals	Subject at school	Drinks

6. Jim e Kate têm preferências diferentes. Complete as frases escolhendo, a seu critério, as opções de cada um.

a) fruit
   Kate: Her favorite fruit is apple.
   Jim: His favorite fruit is mango.

b) animal
   Kate:

   Jim:

c) color
   Kate:

   Jim:

d) food
   Kate:

   Jim:

e) drink
   Kate:

   Jim:

f) music
   Kate:

   Jim:

g) day of the week
   Kate:

   Jim:

h) subject at school
   Kate:

   Jim:

i) friend
   Kate:

   Jim:

7. Responda às questões sobre você.

a) What's your name?

b) What's your father's name?

c) What's your mother's name?

ANOTAÇÕES

d) What's your favorite color?

e) What are your friends' names?

f) What's your favorite sport?

g) What's your favorite fruit?

h) What's your favorite food?

i) What's your favorite subject at school?

j) When is your birthday?

k) Where are you from?

Lesson 14 – Is that your house?

- Is that your house?
- Yes, it's our house.
- May I talk to your father?
- Of course you may. Ring the bell near the door, please.

PRONOMES PESSOAIS **ADJETIVOS POSSESSIVOS**

I	→	my	→	(meu, minha, meus, minhas)
You	→	your	→	(seu, sua, seus, suas)
He	→	his	→	(dele, seu, sua, seus, suas)
She	→	her	→	(dela, seu, sua, seus, suas)
It	→	its	→	(dele, dela, seu, sua, seus, suas)
We	→	our	→	(nosso, nossa, nossos, nossas)
You	→	your	→	(seu, sua, seus, suas)
They	→	their	→	(deles, delas, seu, sua, seus, suas)

1. Siga o modelo.

(house – blue)
– What color is your house?
– Our house is blue.

a) (car – black)

b) (ball – red)

2. Siga o modelo:

His pullover is red. Her pullover is red, too.
Their pullovers are red.

a) His house is small. Her house is small, too.

b) His car is new. Her car is new, too.

c) His child is nice. Her child is nice, too.

d) His teacher is good. Her teacher is good, too.

e) His father is old. Her father is old, too.

3. Escreva as frases no plural:

a) His house is new.

b) His car is red.

c) Her house is modern.

d) My pencil is black.

e) Your shirt is white.

4. Complete com pronomes possessivos, siga o modelo.

I am Spanish. **My** name is Pablo.

a) You are Brazilian. _____ name is José.

b) She is American. _____ name is Liza.

c) He is Portuguese. _____ name is Joaquim.

d) That is my dog. _____ name is Flash.

e) They are English. _____ names are Steve and Grace.

f) We are Italian. _____ names are Gina and Bruno.

g) Mary, sign _____ name here, please.

h) Let's phone _____ friends in Brazil.

i) This book is in _____ first edition.

j) I am sure of _____ decision.

k) These are _____ parents. _____ names are James and Barbara.

l) Open _____ books, please.

m) Frank and _____ sister are at school.

n) Diana is with _____ boyfriend in the park.

o) Sam and Liz phone _____ parents every day.

p) What's the title of the book that you are reading? _____ title is *Save the Earth*.

ANOTAÇÕES

Review – Lessons 11, 12, 13 and 14

1. Complete com os pronomes **his**, **her** ou **their**.

a) Charles –
b) Jane –
c) John and Mary –
d) Davis –
e) Alfred –
f) Susan –
g) Ann and Paul –
h) Mary –
i) Rose and Betty –

2. Complete com os pronomes **his** ou **her**.

a) Jane has a new car. (has: tem) _____ car is blue.

b) Paul has a new bike. _____ bike is red.

c) Fred has a house. _____ house is big.

d) Meg has a beautiful shirt. _____ shirt is white.

e) Betty has many books. _____ books are interesting.

3. Traduza para o inglês.

a) A casa delas é linda.

b) A casa delas é nova.

c) Estes são os livros dele.

d) Estes são os livros deles.

e) Aquelas são as amigas dela.

4. Traduza o imperativo afirmativo para inglês.

a) Espere um momento.

b) Pare o carro.

c) Vire à direita.

d) Feche a porta.

5. Escreva no imperativo negativo.

a) Open the windows.

b) Please close the door.

c) Come here, please.

d) Go away!

e) Turn left.

Leia o texto e traduza, use o word bank

HERE ARE SOME TIPS TO BE A SAFE SKATER

1. Wear a helmet if you are not good in skating. Concrete and rocks are very hard and you can hurt your head.
2. Wear knee and elbow pads.
3. Wear gloves to protect your hands.
4. Don't wear clothes that can hold your movements.
5. Take care of your skates. You can get hurt if you don't pay attention to safety.

WORD BANK
some tips: algumas dicas
to be: para ser
safe: seguro
skater: aquele que anda de patins
wear: use, vista
helmet: capacete
if you are not: se você não é
rocks: pedras
very hard: muito duro
can hurt: podem machucar
head: cabeça
knee pad: joelheira
elbow pad: cotoveleira
gloves: luvas
hands: mãos
don't wear: não use
clothes: roupas
that can: que possam
hold: prender
you can get hurt: você pode se machucar
if you don't pay attention: se você não prestar atenção
to safety: para a segurança

Dictation

6. Ouça com atenção o ditado que o professor vai apresentar e escreva.

ANOTAÇÕES

Lesson 15 – Prepositions of place

- Give me a lift, please!
- Where are you going?
- I'm going to Rio.
- And where are you coming from?
- I'm coming from São Paulo.
- OK! Sit between my son and my brother, please.
- Thank you very much.

PREPOSIÇÕES

1. **From**: de, desde
   From indica origem, procedência, começo
   I'm coming **from** São Paulo.
2. **To**: para
   To indica destino, fim de uma ação (I'm going **to** Rio.)
   (I work from one o'clock **to** seven o'clock.)
3. **Between**: entre dois seres ou dois grupos de seres
   (I am **between** Mary and John.)
4. **Among**: entre, no meio de muitos (I am **among** friends.)
5. **In**: em, dentro (The eggs are **in** the basket).
6. **On**: sobre (The books are **on** the table.)
7. **Under**: debaixo de (The dog is **under** the table.)
8. **Near**: perto de (She lives **near** you.)
9. **Far from**: longe de (I live **far from** the school.)
10. **In front of**: na frente de (She lives **in front of** me.)
11. **Behind**: atrás de (Deborah sits **behind** Fred.)
12. **Over**: acima de (The kite is **over** the house.)
13. **Below**: abaixo de (He is fishing **below** the bridge.)

1. Observe as figuras e responda às perguntas empregando as preposições da página anterior.

a) Where is Jane sitting?

b) Where is the bus going to?

c) Where is Michael Jackson?
Michael Jackson is
( ) behind the people.
( ) between the people.
( ) among the people.
( ) far from the people.
( ) near the people.

d) Where is the baby monkey? Is under/on its mother?

e) Where are the chicks?

f) Is Brazil near or far from Bolivia?

g) Is Japan near or far from Brazil?

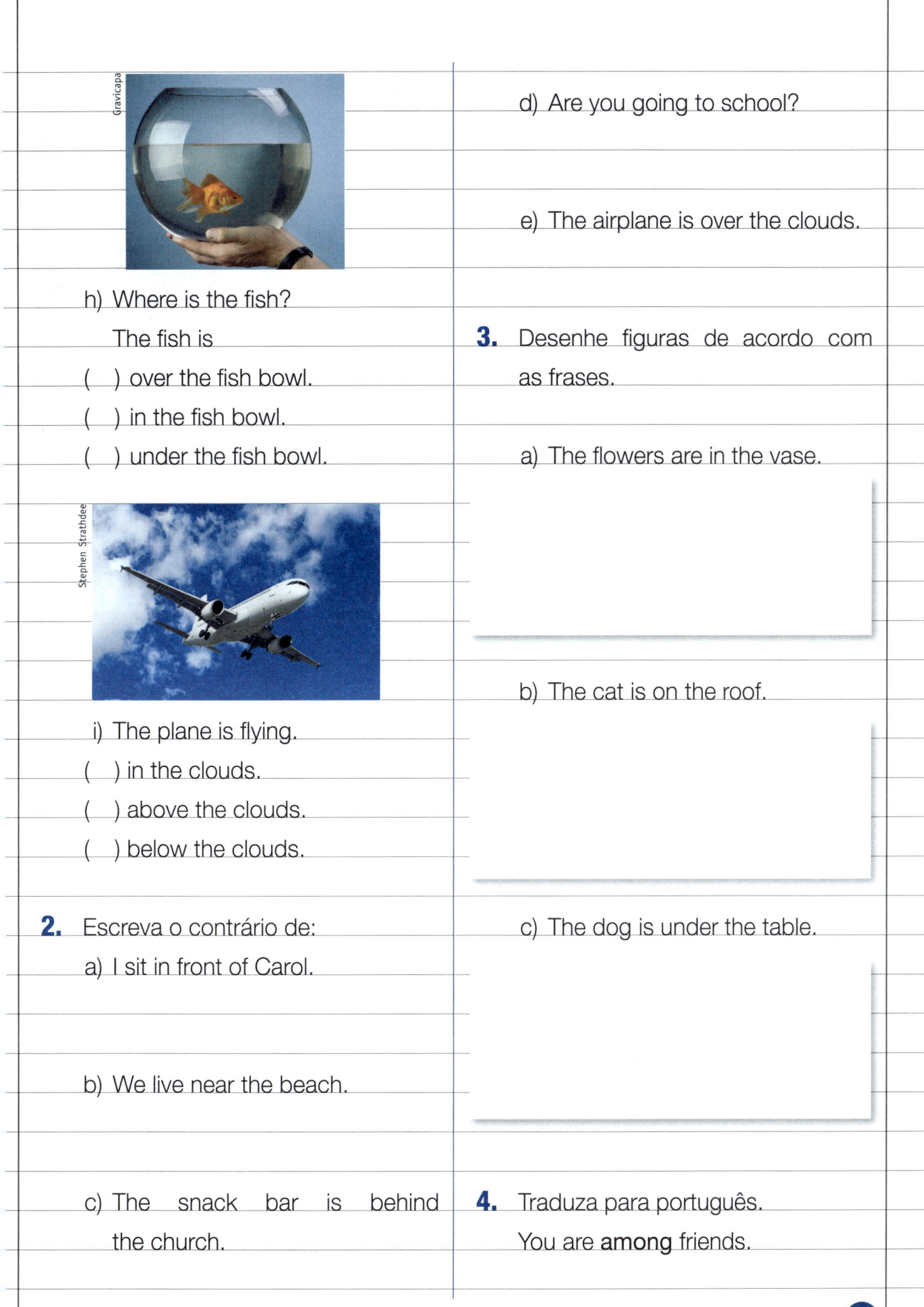

h) Where is the fish?
   The fish is
   ( ) over the fish bowl.
   ( ) in the fish bowl.
   ( ) under the fish bowl.

i) The plane is flying.
   ( ) in the clouds.
   ( ) above the clouds.
   ( ) below the clouds.

2. Escreva o contrário de:
   a) I sit in front of Carol.

   b) We live near the beach.

   c) The snack bar is behind the church.

   d) Are you going to school?

   e) The airplane is over the clouds.

3. Desenhe figuras de acordo com as frases.

   a) The flowers are in the vase.

   b) The cat is on the roof.

   c) The dog is under the table.

4. Traduza para português.
   You are **among** friends.

Our complete address

– We live in a house.
– Where is our house?
– It is in a street.
– Where is the street?
– Our street is in a city.
– Where is our city?
– It is in a state.
– Where is our state?
– Our state is in a country.
– Where is the country?
– It is in a continent.
– And where is the continent?
– Our continent is on Planet Earth.
– And... where is Planet Earth?
– The Earth is in the Solar System.
It's a blue planet that orbits around the Sun, in the wide universe.
This is our spacial address!

5. From your house to the universe

1. You live
( ) in a house ( ) in an apartment

2. What's the name of your street?

3. What's the name of your city?

4. The name of your state is

5. What's the name of your country?

6. The name of your continent is

7. The name of your planet is

8. Our Planet Earth is in the

9. Planet Earth orbits around the
in the wide

Lesson 16 – Numbers

SCORE BOARD				
Brazil	5	x	1	Argentina
Italy	2	x	1	Spain
Japan	2	x	0	England
US	0	x	2	Germany
World Champion – Brazil				

NUMBERS

1. one
2. two
3. three
4. four
5. five
6. six
7. seven
8. eight
9. nine
10. ten
11. eleven
12. twelve
13. thir**teen**
14. four**teen**
15. fif**teen**
16. six**teen**
17. seven**teen**
18. eigh**teen**
19. nine**teen**
20. twen**ty**
21. twen**ty**-one
22. twen**ty**-two
23. twen**ty**-three
30. thir**ty**
31. thir**ty**-one
40. for**ty**
50. fif**ty**
60. six**ty**
70. seven**ty**
80. eigh**ty**
90. nine**ty**
100. **one** hundred or **a** hundred
101. **one** hundred and one
120. **one** hundred and twenty
200. **two** hundred
201. **two** hundred and one
300. **three** hundred
400. **four** hundred
500. **five** hundred
600. **six** hundred
700. **seven** hundred
800. **eight** hundred
900. **nine** hundred
1000. **one** thousand

Nota: depois da palavra **hundred**, (cem, cento) usar **and**

1. Escreva os números correspondentes a cada figura:

> **Observação:**
>
> Forma-se o plural dos substantivos em inglês geralmente acrescentando-se o **s**: car – cars
> girl – girls
> ball – balls
> boy – boys
> house – houses

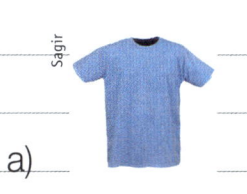

a) T-shirt

b)  trees

c)  icecreams

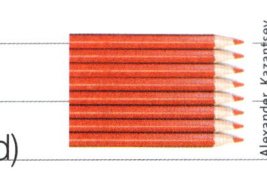

d) pencils

e) 

Dmytro Pauk

bananas

f) 

Zoonar RF

kites

g) 

Victor Habbick

rings

h) 

Jan Sandvik

shoes

i) 

Ivonne Wierink

flowers

j) 

101imges

hats

2. Escreva estes números em inglês.

9
12
3
17
8
2
10
6
7
1
20

VERB TO HAVE (TER)

I have (eu tenho)
You have (você tem)
He, she, it has (ele, ela tem)
We have (nós temos)
You have (vocês têm)
They have (eles, elas têm)

3. Siga o modelo:

I – 2 brothers.

I have two brothers.

a) You – 3 sisters

b) We – 5 friends

c) They – 6 cars

d) He – 4 toys

e) she – 9 belts

f) Rose and Anna – 2 bicycles

g) Mary – 2 shirts

Lesson 17 – How many...?

INTERROGATIVE EXPRESSIONS:

How many: quantos, quantas
Verbo haver (afirmativo):
There is: há (singular)
There are: há (plural)

Verbo haver (interrogativo)
Is there?: há? (singular)
Are there?: há? (plural)

1. Observe a figura e responda:

a) How many boys are there in the picture?

b) How many girls are there in the picture?

c) How many cars are there in the picture?

d) How many bicycles are there in the picture?

e) And birds? How many birds are there in the picture?

f) And trees? How many trees are there in the picture?

g) And dogs? How many dogs are there in the picture?

2. Continue:

a) Are there ten boys in the picture?

b) Are there five girls in the picture?

c) Are there nine cars in the picture?

d) Is there one motorcycle in the picture?

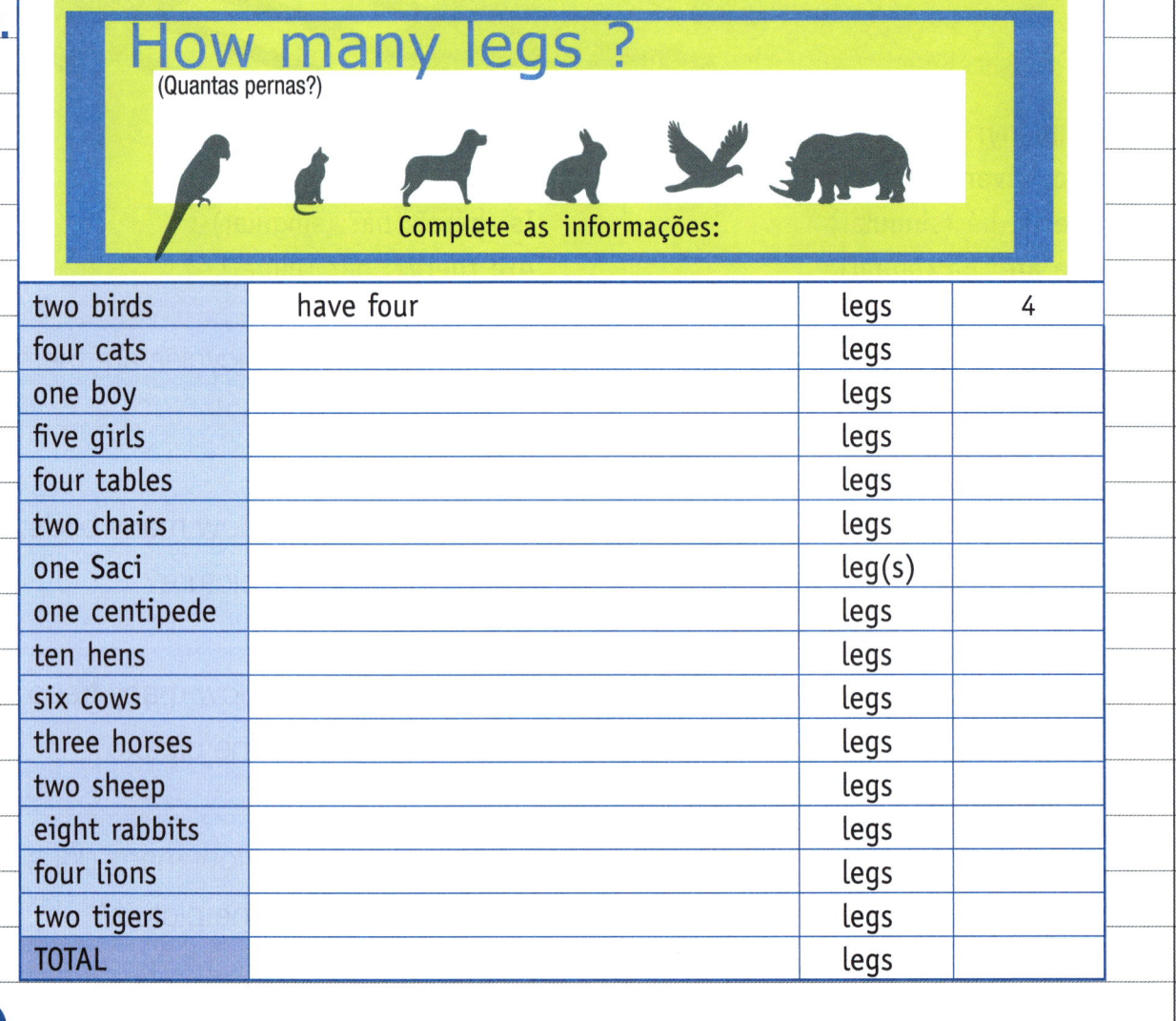

e) Is there one bus in the picture?

f) Are there four girls in the picture?

3. How many legs ?
(Quantas pernas?)

Complete as informações:

two birds	have four	legs	4
four cats		legs	
one boy		legs	
five girls		legs	
four tables		legs	
two chairs		legs	
one Saci		leg(s)	
one centipede		legs	
ten hens		legs	
six cows		legs	
three horses		legs	
two sheep		legs	
eight rabbits		legs	
four lions		legs	
two tigers		legs	
TOTAL		legs	

Lesson 18 – How much...? How many...?

How much are these pants?

They cost thirty dollars.

INTERROGATIVE EXPRESSIONS:

Mrs. Stanley enters a shop.
She wants to buy some clothes.

How much: quanto.
Refere-se a um substantivo no singular, que não podemos quantificar:
How much milk is there in the glass?
(Quanto leite há no copo?)
How many: quantos, quantas.
Refere-se a substantivos no plural, a seres que podemos contar em unidades separadas:
How many cars are there in the street?
(Quantos carros há na rua?)

Observe a conjugação do verbo **to enter**, no presente do indicativo:

I enter	(eu entro)
You enter	(tu entras)
He enters	(ele entra)
She enters	(ela entra)
It enters	(ele/ela entra)
We enter	(nós entramos)
You enter	(vós entrais)
They enter	(eles entram)

Em inglês, a maioria dos verbos recebe **s** na 3ª pessoa do singular do presente do indicativo.

1. Conjugue o verbo amar (**to love**) no presente do indicativo.

2. Traduza diálogo entre a sra. Stanley e a vendedora.

3. Empregue **how much** ou **how many**.

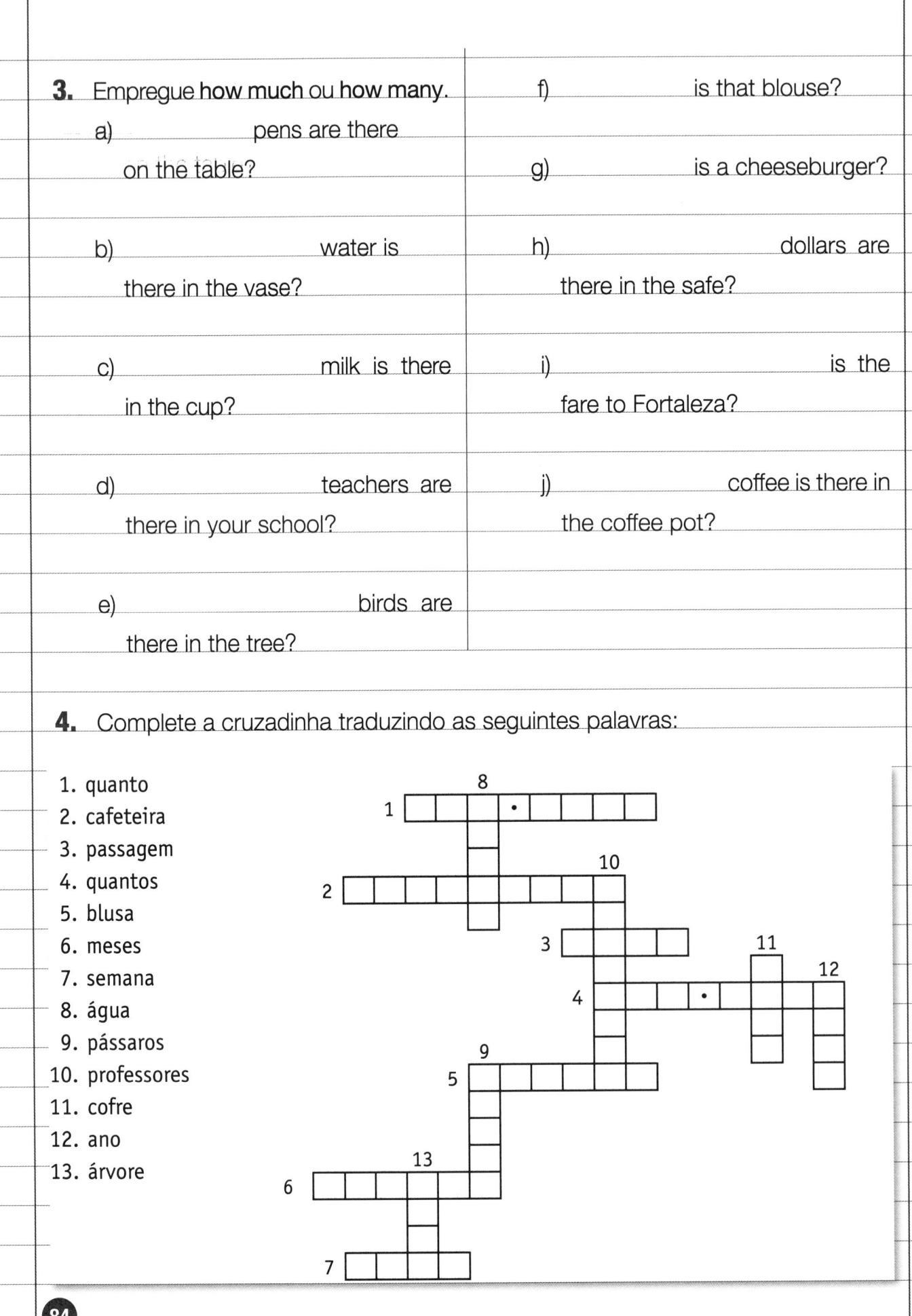

a) _____ pens are there on the table?

b) _____ water is there in the vase?

c) _____ milk is there in the cup?

d) _____ teachers are there in your school?

e) _____ birds are there in the tree?

f) _____ is that blouse?

g) _____ is a cheeseburger?

h) _____ dollars are there in the safe?

i) _____ is the fare to Fortaleza?

j) _____ coffee is there in the coffee pot?

4. Complete a cruzadinha traduzindo as seguintes palavras:

1. quanto
2. cafeteira
3. passagem
4. quantos
5. blusa
6. meses
7. semana
8. água
9. pássaros
10. professores
11. cofre
12. ano
13. árvore

5. How many differences are there in the second picture?

There are _____ differences.

ANOTAÇÕES

Lesson 19 – How old are you?

> Congratulations! How old are you, sir?
>
> How are you so strong?
>
> I am young! I am only seventy years old!
>
> I like natural food!

HOW OLD ARE YOU?

Para perguntar, em inglês, a idade de alguém, usa-se a expressão **how old**.

– **How old are you?**
(Quantos anos você tem?)
– **I am sixteen years old.**
(Eu tenho dezesseis anos.)
– **How old is she?**
(Quantos anos ela tem?)
– **She is sixteen years old.**
(Ela tem dezesseis anos.)

Para expressar idade, o inglês usa o **verbo ser** (**to be**) e não o verbo ter (**to have**):

I am ten years old.
(Eu tenho dez anos.)

She is sixteen years old.
(Ela tem dezesseis anos.)

---

1. Traduza o texto do diálogo.

2. Observe o modelo e faça os exercícios.

Mary / fourteen
– How old is Mary?
– She is fourteen.

a) your mother / twenty-nine

b) your father / forty-two

c) Peter / sixty

d) The teacher / thirty-five

3. Answer.

a) How old are you?

b) How old is your mother?

c) How old is your father?

d) How old is your best friend?

e) How old is your grandfather?

f) How old is your grandmother?

4. Observe a figura:

I am twenty.
I am eighteen.
I am fourteen.
I am ten.
I am five.
I am three.

5. How old are these girls? Atribua idades às meninas, conforme o figura anterior.

6. Desenhe uma menina e escreva o nome em inglês e a idade dela.

Her name is _____.
She is _____.

7. Desenhe um menino e escreva seu nome e idade em inglês.

name is _____ .
He is _____ .

8. Faça o mesmo com um amigo seu.

His name is _____ .
He is _____ .

9. Faça o mesmo com uma amiga.

Her name is _____ .
She is _____ .

10. Desenhe seu animal de estimação e escreva o nome dele.

His/her name is _____ .

Review – Lessons 15, 16, 17, 18 and 19

1. Escreva as frases no plural:
   a) There is a bird in the nest.

   b) There is an egg in the nest.

   c) There is a boy in the classroom.

2. Responda:
   a) How much is the red blouse?
   (ten dollars)

   b) How much is the white shirt?
   (nine dollars)

3. Escreva por extenso o resultado das seguintes somas:

   a) seven and two is =

   b) four and six is =

   c) three and two is =

4. Responda:
   a) How many days are there in a week?

   b) How many hours are there in a day?

   c) How many minutes are there in an hour?

   d) How many seconds are there in a minute?

   e) How many months are there in a year?

   f) How many seasons are there in a year?

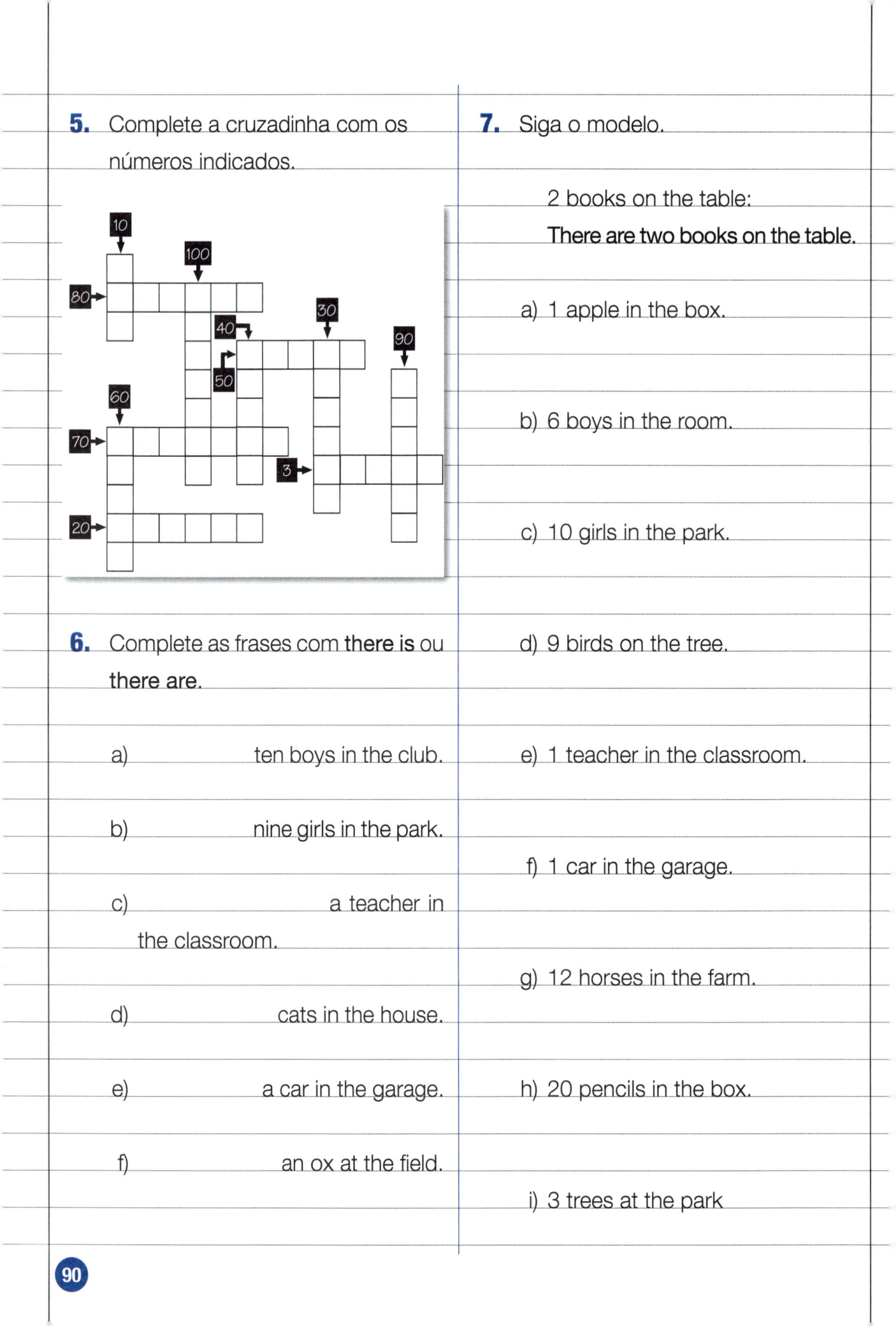

5. Complete a cruzadinha com os números indicados.

6. Complete as frases com **there is** ou **there are**.

a) _____ ten boys in the club.

b) _____ nine girls in the park.

c) _____ a teacher in the classroom.

d) _____ cats in the house.

e) _____ a car in the garage.

f) _____ an ox at the field.

7. Siga o modelo.

2 books on the table:
There are two books on the table.

a) 1 apple in the box.

b) 6 boys in the room.

c) 10 girls in the park.

d) 9 birds on the tree.

e) 1 teacher in the classroom.

f) 1 car in the garage.

g) 12 horses in the farm.

h) 20 pencils in the box.

i) 3 trees at the park

8. Complete as frases com os verbos na 3ª pessoa do singular.

a) Mary is a secretary.
   She _____ letters. (to write)

b) Michael is a singer. He _____ very well. (to sing)

c) Fred loves Rio. He _____ in Rio. (to live)

d) Janet is a good driver.
   She _____ very well.
   (to drive)

e) Alan is a doctor.
   He _____ in a big hospital.
   (to work)

f) Simone is a dancer.
   She _____ very well.
   (to dance)

9. Responda em inglês.

a) How many boys are there in your classroom?

b) How many girls are there in your classroom?

c) How many states are there in Brazil?

d) How many books are there in your schoolbag?

e) How many teachers are there in your school?

f) How much do you like football?

g) How much time do you spend on the computer?

h) How much time do you spend doing homework?

i) How many friends do you have?

Lesson 20 – What time is it? – I

What time is it, please?
It's seven o'clock now.
Thank you!

Telling the time (Falando as horas)
Horas exatas
Observe como se dizem as horas em inglês:
What time is it? (Que horas são?)
It's five o'clock. (São cinco horas.)
It's midday. (É meio-dia.)
It's midnight. (É meia-noite.)
Quando dizemos as horas exatas (sem os minutos), acrescentamos a expressão **o'clock.** (As horas não exatas serão estudadas na próxima lição.)

Quando queremos indicar que se trata de horas antes ou depois do meio-dia, usamos as expressões *ante meridiem* (antes do meio-dia) e *post meridiem* (depois do meio-dia), que são abreviadas **a.m.** e **p.m.** Observe: **It's seven a.m.** (São sete da manhã.) **It's five p.m.** (São cinco da tarde.)
Há outra maneira de perguntar pelas horas: **What's the time?** (Que horas são?)
Na expressão **o'clock, o'** é a contração de **of the:** It's five o'clock = It's five **of the** clock.

1. Traduza o diálogo da figura ao lado:

a) What time is it?

b) What time is it?

2. Observe os relógios e escreva as respostas:

What time is it?
It is twelve o'clock. It's midday. /
It's midnight.

c) What time is it?

d) What time is it?

Lesson 21 – What time is it? – II

– Please, what time is it?
– It's ten past six.
– Thank you.
– You're welcome.

It's five past seven.
It's seven five.

It's fifteen past seven.
It's a quarter past seven.
It's seven fifteen.

It's twenty-five past seven.
It's seven twenty-five.

Telling the time (Falando as horas)
Horas não exatas

Observe os exemplos e aprenda, em inglês, horas não exatas:

It's half past seven.
It's seven thirty.

1. Traduza o diálogo de abertura.

a) What time is it?

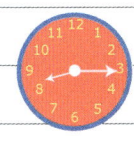

b) What time is it?

2. Observe o modelo e responda.

What time is it?
It's five past seven.
It's seven five.

c) What time is it?

d) What time is it?

3. Desenhe os relógios e ponteiros correspondentes às horas.

a) It's seven o'clock.

b) It's twenty-five past twelve.

c) It's a quarter to twelve.

d) It's a quarter past eight.

4. Relacione a frase com o relógio correspondente.

a) It's nine o'clock.

b) It's two to two.

c) It's five past five. d)

It's ten to ten.

e) It's a quarter past seven. f)

It's half past five.

5. Observe os do relógios e responda.

a) What time is it?

b) What time is it?

c) What time is it?

Additional texts

Introducing people

INTRODUCING A FRIEND

Bill: Good afternoon, Bob.
Bob: Good afternoon.
Bill: Bob, this is my girlfriend Carol.
Bob: Hello, Carol!
Carol: Hello, Bob!
Bob: Bill, congratulations! Carol is a very nice girl.
Carol: Thanks, Bob.
Bob: Where are you going?
Bill: We are going to the movies.
Bob: Well, see you tomorrow.
Bill: Bye.

1. Responda de acordo com o texto.

a) Qual é o nome do amigo de Bill?

b) Com que frase, em inglês, Bill apresentou sua amiga a Bob?

c) Como Bob cumprimenta Carol?

d) Quem está indo para o cinema?

MY FAMILY

I am Paul. I am forty years old. This is my family. There are six people in my family. We are at home now. Our house is not beautiful, but it is large. We are happy in this house.

This is my father.
His name is John.
He is sixty-nine years old.

This is my mother.
Her name is Flavia.
She is sixty-five.

This is Silvia, my wife.
She is thirty-four.

These are my children.
This is my son Mark.
He is only ten years old.

And this is my daughter Mary.
She is fourteen years old.

2. Responda de acordo com o texto.

a) Who is introducing the family?

b) How many people are there in this family?

c) Where are they now?

d) What is Paul's house like?

e) Are they happy?

f) How old is Paul?

g) How old is Paul's father?

h) How old is his mother?

i) And his wife? How old is she?

j) Is Mark a child? How old is he?

3. Responda a respeito de Mary:

a) Who is her father?

b) Who is her mother?

c) Who is her brother?

d) Who is her grandfather?

e) Who is her grandmother?

A GOOD STUDENT

I am Mary. I like to study, to read and to write. I like my school and my teacher very much and when I grow up I want to be a good teacher.

4. Responda às perguntas em inglês e, em seguida, traduza as respostas.

a) A menina do texto gosta de fazer três coisas. Quais são elas?

b) A menina gosta da escola e da professora?

c) O que a menina quer ser quando crescer?

Hotel reception

Woman: Good evening.
Man: Good evening.
Woman: My name is Patricia Bennet.
Man: OK, Mrs Bennet. Welcome to London Hotel! Your room number is 62. Here is the key to the room.

5. Responda em inglês:

a) Qual é o nome da pessoa que está à procura de um quarto num hotel?

b) Qual é o nome do hotel em que ela está?

c) Em que parte do dia sra. Bennet se apresentou no hotel?

d) Como se diz bem-vindo em inglês?

e) Escreva por extenso, em inglês, o número do quarto onde a sra. Bennet vai ficar.

Giving information

Tourist: Excuse me. I'm not from here. I want some information. Can you help me?
Policeman: Yes. I can help you. What's the matter?
Tourist: Please read this address. Where is this street?
Policeman: It's far from here. You must take bus number two.
Tourist: Where's the bus stop?
Policeman: There, in front of the New York Bank.
Tourist: Thank you very much.
Policeman: Nothing at all.

6. Responda em inglês.

a) Quais pessoas estão dialogando no texto?

b) Com que frase o policial diz que pode ajudar a turista?

c) Com que frase o policial diz que a rua é longe dali?

d) Escreva a frase com a qual a turista agradece ao policial.

e) Traduza a frase "Where is the bus stop?"

b) Que rua a menina está procurando?

c) Quantos minutos ela vai demorar para chegar a Palm Street?

d) Represente com um desenho "traffic lights".

Asking for information

SEARCHING A STREET
Girl: Excuse me. Can you tell me where Palm Street is?
Boy: Yes, of course. Walk to the traffic lights. Palm Street crosses this street at the traffic lights.
Girl: Are the traffic lights far?
Boy: No, just five minutes from here.
Girl: Thank you very much. Goodbye.
Boy: Goodbye.

7. Responda em inglês.

a) Quem está dialogando no texto?

At the railway station

TAKING A TRAIN
Woman: Excuse me. What time is the next train to New York?
Attendant: The train leaves at 11 o'clock. Platform 8.
Woman: One ticket, please.
Attendant: Here you are.
Woman: How much is it?
Attendant: It costs five dollars.
Woman: OK. Where is platform 8?
Attendant: Platform 8 is right in front of you.
Woman: Thank you.

8. Responda as perguntas.

a) What time is the next train to New York?

b) How much is the ticket?

Taking a taxi

Woman: Taxi, please.
Driver: Good morning, madam.
Woman: Good morning. Shopping Center Eldorado, please. I must be there at 10 o'clock. I have an important appointment.
Driver: OK, madam. I can drive fast.
Driver: Here we are, madam. It's 10 o'clock.
Woman: Fine! We are in time. You are a good driver. How much is it?
Driver: Two dollars and eighty cents.
Woman: Take three dollars. You can keep the change.
Driver: Thanks, madam.
Woman: Goodbye.
Driver: Goodbye.

9. Responda em inglês.

a) A que horas a mulher deve chegar ao shopping?

b) Escreva o trecho em que a mulher elogia o motorista.

c) Com que frase ela pergunta: "Quanto custa"?

10. Escreva **true** ou **false**.

a) The woman is going to the shopping center. (   )

b) The taxi driver is a good driver. (   )

c) The taxi driver drives slowly. (   )

Geraldo Resende

My name is Geraldo Resende. I am twenty years old. I am from Minas Gerais but now I live in São Paulo with my sister. I go to work by bus every day. I work in a big shop downtown. I sell clothes for men. I like my job very much.

11. Responda em inglês.

a) What is the man's name?

b) How old is he?

c) Where is he from?

12. Assinale as alternativas corretas:

( ) Geraldo is from Minas Gerais.
( ) He lives in São Paulo with his brother.
( ) He lives in São Paulo with his sister.
( ) He goes to work by car.
( ) He goes to work by bus.
( ) He works in a small shop.
( ) He sells clothes for women.
( ) He sells clothes for men.
( ) He works in a big shop downtown.
( ) He likes his job very much.

13. Be a good cyclist.

Relacione as frases em inglês com a sua tradução em português.

(a) Cycling is a good sport.
(b) Cross intersections with care.
(c) Obey traffic laws.
(d) Signs are for bike riders, too.
(e) Keep to the right.
(f) Ride single file.
(g) Use both hands to control your bike.
(h) Don't do tricks in traffic.
(i) Keep off highways.

( ) Atravesse os cruzamentos com cuidado.
( ) O ciclismo é um bom esporte.
( ) Obedeça às leis de trânsito.
( ) Mantenha-se à direita.
( ) Ande em fila única.
( ) Os sinais de trânsito são para ciclistas também.
( ) Fique longe das estradas.
( ) Use ambas as mãos para controlar sua bicicleta.
( ) Não faça brincadeiras no tráfego.

WORD BANK
route: rota
lane: pista
slowly: devagar
caution: cuidado, precaução
watch: observe, veja
yield: dar preferência
pedestrian: pedestre

Go Slowly
Respect Others

CYCLISTS YIELD TO PEDESTRIANS

BIKE ROUTE

Crosswords

14. Enriqueça seu vocabulário de inglês sobre o trânsito.

1. Estrada
2. Ciclista
3. Cuidado
4. Rua
5. Sinais
6. Lei
7. Estacionamento
8. Cruzar
9. Rodovia
10. Regras, normas
11. Pare
12. Tráfego

Water

Today scientists say that liquid water is indispensable for life.

Water is a liquid.
There is liquid water in river, lakes and oceans. And in the rain.

Water is a gas.
It is called water vapor, the vapor rises and forms the clouds.
When water vapor cools, it falls as rain.

Water is solid.
Solid water is ice.

15. According to the text:

1 Ice is
( ) liquid water ( ) solid water

2. The rain is
( ) solid water ( ) liquid water.

3. The water vapor rises and forms clouds
( ) Yes ( ) No

4. Igloos are made from ice.
( ) False ( ) True

5. When vapor cools, it falls as rain.
( ) Yes ( ) No

6. Liquid water is indispensable for life.
( ) True ( ) False

16. Leia os textos e traduza em seguida:

Seasons (Estações)

There are four seasons in a year. They are: **spring, summer, autumn** (or **fall**) and **winter**.

Spring – Is the season of flowers. There are green trees and birds singing everywhere. In spring, nature is very beautiful.

Autumn (or **fall**) – Is the season of fruit. The wind blows and the leaves fall from the trees.

Summer – Is a hotseason. The sun shines brightly. People go to the beach or to a swimming pool.

Winter – Winter is a cold season. It snows in Europe and North America and in other countries in the world.

Jobs

Adam meets Mary on the bus

Adam: Hello, Mary!
Mary: Hello!
Adam: Are you still a secretary?
Mary: No, now I'm a teacher of Arts.
Adam: Where are you teaching Arts?
Mary: I'm teaching Arts near my home, at Modern Arts School.
Adam: Oh, that's fine! I like Arts.
Mary: And you, Adam? What's your job?
Adam: Now I'm studying Medicine. I spend all the time studying.
Mary: Studying all the time?
Adam: No! On the weekends I practice sports, I go to the movies, to the beach, I meet friends...
Mary: Excuse me... Adam... I must get off now. So long.
Adam: So long.

In a supermarket

Wife: John, we have no sugar, no bread, no coffee, no butter, no rice, no beans, no vegetables...

Husband: What else?

Wife: Bring also milk, cheese, soda, tomatoes and meat.

Husband: Well! I'm going to search all these things.

Husband: Clerk, please. Can you deliver all these things to my house?

Clerk: Certainly! What's your address?

Husband: Liberty Street, 10.

Clerk: OK.

Husband: Thank you.

Telephoning I

Mary: Hello! Mary here. Please, can I speak to Jane?
Paul: Yes. Wait a moment, please. (The boy looks for Jane in the house.)
Paul: Mary, I'm sorry! Jane is out. She comes at midday.
Mary: Thank you! I'll call later.

Telephoning II

Wrong number
Jane: Hello! This is Janet. Can I speak to Paul?
Telephonist: Paul? There is no Paul here!
Jane: Please, what's your telephone number?
Telephonist: My telephone number is 12507 (one, two, five, zero, seven).
Jane: Isn't it number 12607 (one, two, six, zero, seven)?
Telephonist: No, here is number 12507.
Jane: I'm sorry, excuse me.
Telephonist: OK.

Fun time – Divirta-se aprendendo

1. Complete a cruzadinha de acordo com as figuras:

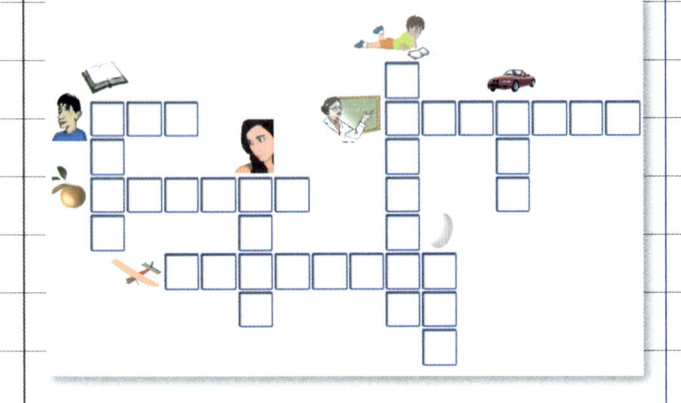

2. Desembaralhe as palavras abaixo:

a) ybo

b) koob

c) rigl

d) geg

3. Veja a figura do arco-íris e relacione as colunas entre si.

rain	arco
bow	chuva
rainbow	nuvem
cloud	arco-íris
sky	céu
umbrella	menina
girl	guarda-chuva

4. Encontre no (caça-palavras) word hunt as palavras abaixo:

season – year – tree – spring
flower – green

```
W U N K N O P E S K Z E X
M I N S E A S O N V W O P
X C I T E O K E I E A H I
N X E T R E E P C Q Ç A X
S H D L W E S N V I O P N
X L S P R I N G Q R T I K
V X N N U A V I Y S L A Q
N R Y E A R L W Q A C V B
S Y N A R O E S M H M R O
F L O W E R C H O O L S Y
D B Y I S W A D L O S N X
K J L F O G R E E N V L P
Z X C V B C H M U I E S Y
```

RAINBOW = ARCO-ÍRIS
RAIN = CHUVA
BOW = ARCO
CLOUD = NUVENS

5. Traduza a música.

One, two.

Buckle my shoe.

Three, four.

Open the door.

Five, six.

Pick up sticks.

Seven, eight.

Open the gate.

Nine, ten.

A big fat hen.

7. Escreva os números de um a dez:

8. Complete the faces. (Desenhe os rostos: o menino com cara de bravo e a menina feliz.)

An angry boy.

A happy girl.

9. How many differences are there in the pictures below? (Quantas diferenças há nas imagens abaixo?)

a) There are _____ differences.

b) There are _____ differences.

10. Follow the lines and mark the correct answer to each picture.
(Siga as linhas e assinale a resposta correta para cada figura.)

House   1) ( )   2) ( )   3) ( )

Dog   1) ( )   2) ( )   3) ( )

Goalkeeper 1) ( )   2) ( )   3) ( )

11. Are you a good observer? Find out five things that are wrong in this crazy office.

12. Match trick

By changing the position of just two of these matches, see if you can form a new arrangement made up of only two squares.

13. Look alikes

Only two of these butterflies are exactly alike. Can you spot the twins?

14. Complete the beginning or the ending of each word.

og   go

oo   ca

at   ig

ff   tt

15. Find the things that are too large in this picture.

The things that are too large in the picture are:

WORD BANK
too much: exagerado, demais
find: encontre
fireplace: lareira
knife: faca
match: fósforo
cup: xícara
lamp: lâmpada
spoon: colher
fork: garfo

ANOTAÇÕES

General vocabulary

A

a, an: um, uma
about: sobre, a respeito, aproximadamente
above: acima
address: endereço
afraid of: com medo de
after: depois
afternoon: tarde
again: de novo
age: idade
airplane: avião
alike: semelhante, igual
all: todo, todos, toda, todas
also: também
always: sempre
am: sou, estou
among: entre (muitos)
and: e
angry: bravo
ant: formiga
any: qualquer
apple: maçã
appointment: encontro
are: são, estão, é, está, somos, estamos
around: em volta, em torno
arrangement: arranjo, disposição
arrival: chegada
arrive: chegar
arrogant: arrogante
as: como
ask: pedir, perguntar
ask for some information: pedir algumas informações
astronaut: astronauta
at: em, no, na, nos, nas
attentive: atento
at the: no, na, nos, nas
at home: em casa
at the beach: na praia
autumn: outono
away: embora; longe

B

baby: bebê
bad: ruim, mau
bag: mala
ball: bola
basket: cesta
bathroom: banheiro
be: ser, estar
beach: praia
beans: feijões
beautiful: bonito
bed: cama
bedroom: quarto
beer: cerveja
begins: começa, inicia
behind: atrás

bell: sino, campainha
belong: pertencer
below: embaixo, abaixo, debaixo
belt: cinto
best: melhor
between: entre (dois)
bicycle, bike: bicicleta
big: grande
bird: pássaro
birth: nascimento
birthday: aniversário
bite: morder
black: preto
blackboard: lousa (quadro-negro)
blond: loiro
blonde: loira
blouse: blusa
blue: azul
boat: barco
book: livro
bookshop: livraria
both: ambos
box: caixa
boy: menino, rapaz
boyfriend: namorado
bread: pão
breakfast: café da manhã, desjejum
bridge: ponte
bring: trazer
brother: irmão
brown: marrom, moreno, castanho

buckle: fivela, afivelar
bus: ônibus
bus station: estação de ônibus
bus stop: parada de ônibus
but: mas, porém
butter: manteiga
butterfly: borboleta
button: abotoar
buy: comprar
by: por

C

cake: bolo
call: chamar (called: chamado)
can: poder
candy: bala, doce
can you see: você pode ver?
car: carro
care: cuidado
cat: gato
cellphone: telefone móvel, celular
cent: centavo
centipede: centopeia
certainly: certamente
chair: cadeira
chalk: giz
chalkboard: quadro de giz
change: troco, trocar
changing: mudando, trocando
chair: cadeira
cheap: barato

cheese: queijo
chick: pinto, pintinho
chicken: frango
child: criança
children: crianças, filhos
Chinese: chinês
Christmas: Natal
Christmas tree: árvore de Natal
church: igreja
city: cidade
class: classe
classmate: colega de classe
clean: limpo, limpar
clerk: funcionário, empregado, atendente
clock: relógio de parede
close: fechar, feche
cloud: nuvem
clothes: roupas
coat: paletó
coffee: café
coffee pot: bule, cafeteira
color, colour: cor
coin: moeda
comb: pente
come: vir, venha
come back: voltar
come from: vir de
comfortable: confortável
computing: computação
congratulations: parabéns

cook: cozinheiro, cozinhar
cools: esfria, resfria
copybook: caderno
corner: canto, esquina
cost: custar
cotton: algodão
country: país
countries: países
cow: vaca
crazy: louco, doido, maluco
cross: cruz, cruzar, atravessar
cry: chorar, gritar
cup: xícara
cyclist: ciclista

D

dad: papai
dancer: dançarino
dangerous: perigoso
date: encontro
daughter: filha
day: dia
dear: querido(a)
deceive: enganar
December: dezembro
decision: decisão
delicious: delicioso
deliver: entregar
delivery: entrega
dice: dados
die: morrer, dado

difference: diferença
dinner: jantar
dining room: sala de jantar
dirty: sujo
disabled: deficiente, incapacitado
do: fazer
doing: fazendo
doctor: médico, doutor
dog: cão
donkey: burro, jumento
don't: não
door: porta
dotted: pontuado
downstairs: andar térreo
downtown: centro da cidade
draw: desenhar, desenhe, traçar, trace
drawing: desenhando, desenho
dress: vestido
drink: beber, beba; bebida
drive: dirigir, dirija
driver: motorista
dry: secar

E

each: cada
early: cedo
ears: orelhas
Earth: Terra
easy: fácil
eat: comer, coma
edition: edição

egg: ovo
eight: oito
eighteen: dezoito
eighty: oitenta
end: fim
ending: fim, final
engineer: engenheiro
England: Inglaterra
English: inglês
enter: entrar
erase: apagar
evening: anoitecer, entardecer, noite
every: cada, todo, todos
everybody (everyone): todo mundo
everywhere: por toda parte
excellent: excelente
excuse me: desculpe-me, com licença
expensive: caro
eye: olho

F

factory: fábrica
fall: cair, queda, outono (cair das folhas)
false: falso
family: família
far: longe
far from: longe de
fare: passagem, bilhete
farm: fazenda
farmer: fazendeiro

fast: rápido
fat: gordo
father: pai
February: fevereiro
fifteen: quinze
fifty: cinquenta
file: arquivo, lista, ficha, fichário
fine: bem (I'm fine: estou me bem)
find: encontrar, encontre
find out: descobrir, descubra
fireman: bombeiro
first: primeiro
fish: peixe, pescar
fishing: pescando
fisherman: pescador
five: cinco
flash: clarão, flash de câmera fotográfica, brilho intenso
flower: flor
fly: voar, voo, pilotar avião
flying: voando
follow: seguir, siga
food: comida, alimento
football: futebol
for: para, por
forest: floresta
fork: garfo
forty: quarenta
four: quatro
fourteen: catorze, quatorze
fox: raposa

French: francês
Friday: sexta-feira
friend: amigo, amiga
friends' names: nomes dos amigos
from: de, desde

G

galaxy: galáxia
garage: garagem
garden: jardim
gardener: jardineiro
gas: gás, gasolina
gate: portão
geese: gansos
gentleman: cavalheiro
German: alemão
Germany: Alemanha
get: ganhar, receber, chegar, comprar, conseguir, obter
get off: sair, saia
get out: sair, saia
get up: levantar
girl: menina, moça
girlfriend: namorada
giraffe: girafa
give: dar
glass: copo, vidro
go: ir, vá
go away: vá embora
going: indo
goal: objetivo, baliza, meta, fim; gol

goalkeeper: goleiro
good: bom, boa, bons, boas
good afternoon: boa tarde
goodbye: adeus, até logo
good evening: boa noite (ao cumprimentar à noite)
good morning: bom dia
good night: boa noite (ao se despedir à noite)
goose: ganso
grandfather: avô
grandmother: avó
great: grande, ótimo
green: verde
greetings: saudações, cumprimentos
grey, gray: cinza, cinzento
grow up: crescer

H

hair: cabelo
half: meio, metade
hall: sala de entrada
hand: mão
happy: feliz
has: tem
hat: chapéu
have: ter
he: ele
head: cabeça
headache: dor de cabeça
heavy: pesado, intenso
hello: alô, oi
help: socorro, ajudar, ajude...
hen: galinha
her: dela, seu, sua, seus, suas
here: aqui
here you are: aqui está
hi: oi, olá
hidden: escondido
highway: rodovia
his: dele, seu, sua, seus, suas
hobby: passatempo
home: casa, lar
horse: cavalo
hot: quente, com calor
house: casa
hour: hora
how: como
how are you?: como vai você?
how many?: quantos?
how much?: quanto?
how old?: que idade?

I

I: eu
ice: gelo
If: se
I'm: eu sou, eu estou
I'm going: eu vou, eu estou indo
I'm sorry: sinto muito, desculpe-me
in: em, dentro
in front of: em frente de

information: informações, informação
is: é, está
in it: no, na, nele, nela
interesting: interessante
introducing: apresentando
it: ele, ela, o, a
its: seu, sua
it's: ele é, ele está, ela é, ela está, é
Italian: italiano

J

January: janeiro
Japan: Japão
Japanese: japonês
job: emprego, trabalho
juice: suco
just: apenas, somente, exatamente

K

keep: guardar, guarde
keep off: fique fora
keep the change: fique com o troco
key: chave
kick: chutar, chute
king: rei
kitchen: cozinha
kite: pipa, papagaio, raia
knife: faca
knives: facas

L

lake: lago
lamp: lâmpada
large: grande, amplo
last: último
late: atrasado, tarde
later: mais tarde
law: lei
lazy: preguiçoso
leader: líder
leaf: folha
leaves: folhas
leaving: partindo, deixando
left: esquerda
leg: perna
lemon: limão
let: deixar, deixe
let's: vamos
let's sing: vamos cantar
letter: carta, letra
lift: carona
light: luz; leve (traffic lights: semáforo)
like: gostar
listen: escutar
little: pequeno
life: vida
lion: leão
live: viver, morar
lives: vidas
living room: sala de estar
long: comprido, longo

London: Londres
look at: olhar para, olhe para
look for: procurar
loud: alto
love: amor, amar
lunch: almoço
lunch time: hora do almoço

M

madam: madame, senhora
made: feito
made up: composto de, feito de
magazine: revista
mailman: carteiro
make: fazer, fabricar
man: homem (men: homens)
mango: manga
many: muitos, muitas
market: mercado
marvelous: maravilhoso
match: fósforo, combinar, combine, jogo
matter: material, assunto, problema
may: poder, pode, posso...
me eu
meal: refeição
meat: carne
meet: encontrar, conhecer, encontro
mess: bagunça
Mexican: mexicano
mice: ratos (mouse: rato)

midday: meio-dia
midnight: meia-noite
milk: leite
minute: minuto
Miss: senhorita
miss: falha, perder
modern: moderno
Monday: segunda-feira
money: dinheiro
monkey: macaco
month: mês
Moon: lua
Mr. [mis-ter]: senhor (Mr e Mrs são usados diante de sobrenomes)
Mrs. [mis-iz]: senhora (tratamento para mulher casada)
morning: manhã
mother: mãe
mother's name: nome da mãe
mouse: rato
move: mudar, mexer, mover
movies: cinema
much: muito, muita
must: precisar, dever, ter de (I must go: eu preciso ir)
my: meu, meus, minha, minhas

N

name: nome
nature: natureza
near: perto de

neck: pescoço
nest: ninho
next: próximo, seguinte
new: novo
newspaper: jornal
nice: ótimo, bom, bonito, bem, bacana
nice to meet you: prazer em conhecê-lo
night: noite
nine: nove
nineteen: dezenove
ninety: noventa
no: não, nenhum
noise: barulho
noisy: barulhento
north: norte
not: não
nothing: nada
nothing at all: de nada
now: agora
number: número

O

occupation: profissão
of: de
of the: dos, das, do, da
office: escritório
office boy: ajudante de escritório
OK: tudo certo
old: velho
on: sobre (on the right: à direita, on the left: à esquerda)

on sale: em oferta
only: somente, apenas
open: abrir
or: ou
orange: laranja
orbit: órbita
other: outro
our: nosso, nossa, nossos, nossas
out: fora
over: em cima
ox: boi
oxen: bois

P

painter: pintor
pair: par
pants: calças
parents: pais
parents': dos pais
parents' name: nome dos pais
park: estacionar, parque
parrot: papagaio
past: passado
pattern: modelo
pay: pagar
peach: pêssego
pear: pera
pen: caneta
pencil: lápis
people: pessoas
phone: telefonar, telefone

pick up: ajuntar, pegar, apanhar
picture: quadro, foto, desenho
pig: porco
pilot: piloto
pink: cor-de-rosa
place: lugar
plane: avião
planet: planeta
play: jogar, diversão
player: jogador
playground: pátio
please: por favor
plumber: encanador
policeman: policial
poor: pobre
postman: carteiro
post-office: correio
Portuguese: português
potato: batata
present: presente
price: preço
pullover: pulôver
put: pôr
put on: vestir
put down: pôr no chão

Q

quarter: quarto (de hora...)

R

rabbit: coelho

rail: trilho
railway: estrada de ferro
rain: chuva
rainy: chuvoso
rainbow: arco-íris
raise: levantar
read: ler
reading: lendo, leitura
ready: pronto
receive: receber
red: vermelho
red-head: ruivo
refrigerator: geladeira
registration: registro
rest: descansar, descanso
review: revisão
rice: arroz
rich: rico
ride: cavalgar, montar, corrida
rise: levantar, subir
right: direito, certo (all right: tudo bem/ turn right: vire à direita)
ring the bell: tocar a campainha, tocar o sino
river: rio
road: estrada
roar: urrar
roof: telhado
room: sala, quarto (bedroom: quarto de dormir) (bathroom: banheiro) (living room: sala de estar) (dining room: sala

de jantar)
road: estrada
rose: rosa
rule: regra, norma
ruler: régua
run: correr (runs: corre)
running: correndo

S
sad: triste
safe: cofre
said: disse
sailor: marinheiro
sale: vender (on sale: em oferta)
same: mesmo
Saturday: sábado
save: salvar, economizar
say: dizer, diga
school: escola
schoolbag: mala escolar, mochila
season: estação (do ano)
second: segundo
secretary: secretária
see: ver, veja
sell: vender
set: aparelho
seven: sete
seventeen: dezessete
seventy: setenta
sharpen: apontar
she: ela

sheep: ovelha(s)
shelf: estante
shelves: estantes
shine: brilhar (shines: brilha)
ship: navio
shirt: camisa
shoe: sapato
shop: loja
short: curto, baixo
show: mostrar
shut: fechar, feche
sick: doente
sign: assinar, sinal
signal: sinal; indicar, fazer sinais
sing: cantar
singer: cantor
singing: cantando
single: único; solteiro
sink: afundar
sir: senhor
sister: irmã
sit: sentar
sit down: sente-se, sentar
sitting: sentando
six: seis
sixteen: dezesseis
sixty: sessenta
skin: pele
skirt: saia
sky: céu
skyscraper: arranha-céu

sleep: dormir
small: pequeno
smart: esperto, inteligente
smoke: fumar
soccer: futebol
sock: meia
so: tão
so long: até logo
some: algum, alguma, alguns, algumas, um pouco
something: algo, alguma coisa
son: filho
song: música, canção
soon: cedo, logo
south: sul
sorry: perdão
spaceship: nave espacial
speak: falar
spot: apontar, localizar
spring: primavera
square: quadrado, praça
state: estado
stall: banca
stand: banca, estande
star: estrela
start: começar, início
station: estação (bus station: estação de ônibus)
stick: bengala, bastão
still: ainda
stop: parar (bus stop: ponto de ônibus)
story: estória, conto
stove: fogão
strange: estranho
street: rua
strong: forte
student: estudante
subject: matéria, assunto
substitute: substituir
sugar: açúcar
summer: verão
Sun: Sol
sunflower: girassol
sure: certo, certamente, com certeza
surname: sobrenome
sweet: doce
swim: nadar
swimming: nadando
swimming pool: piscina
Swiss: suíço

T

table: mesa
tail: rabo
take: pegar, pegue, tomar, tome, levar
take away: levar embora
take a taxi: pegar um táxi
take a train: pegar um trem
take off: tirar, remover
talk: conversar
tall: alto

tea: chá
teacher: professor(a)
teaching: ensinando, ensino
team: time
teeth: dentes
tell: contar, dizer
ten: dez
tenth: décimo
terrible: terrível
thanks: obrigado
that: aquele, aquela, aquilo, que
that's easy: isso é fácil
the: o, a, os, as
there: lá
there are: há (plural)
there is: há (singular)
these: estes, estas
they: eles, elas
thief: ladrão
thieves: ladrões
thin: magro
thirteen: treze
thirty: trinta
this: esta, este, isto
those: aqueles
ticket: bilhete, passagem
tidy: em ordem, arrumado
tie: gravata
tiger: tigre
time: tempo
times: vezes

title: título
to: para
to buy: comprar
today: hoje
to eat: comer
to meet: encontrar (pessoas)
tomorrow: amanhã
too: também, demais
tool: ferramenta
too much: demais
tooth: dente
toothbrush: escova de dente
topaz: topázio
to see: ver
touch: tocar
town: cidade
toy: brinquedo
traffic: tráfego
traffic lights: semáforo
train: trem
travel: viajar
tree: árvore
trouble: problema, apuros
trousers: calça
truck: caminhão
true: verdadeiro
Tuesday: terça-feira
turn: virar, turno, vez
turn on: abrir (torneira), acender (fogão)
turn off: fechar (torneira), apagar (fogão)

turn right: virar à direita
turn left: virar à esquerda
twenty: vinte
twelve: doze
twins: gêmeos
two: dois

U

ugly: feio
umbrella: guarda-chuva, sombrinha
unbutton: desabotoar
under: embaixo
upstairs: andar de cima, andar superior
us: nós
usually: geralmente

V

vase: vaso
vegetables: vegetais, verduras, legumes
very: muito
very much: muitíssimo
very well: muito bem

W

wait: esperar, espere
walk: caminhar, caminhe
wall: parede, muro
want: querer, desejar
wash: lavar
watch: assistir; relógio de pulso
water: água
way: caminho, jeito
we: nós
wear: usar (roupas), vestir
weather: tempo, clima
Wednesday: quarta-feira
week: semana
weekend: fim de semana
we have: nós temos
welcome: bem-vindo
well: bem
we're: nós somos, nós estamos
what: o que, qual, quais, que
what else?: o que mais?
what is this?: o que é isso?
what's his house like?: como é a casa dele?
what's the problem/matter?: qual é o problema/assunto?
what do you do?: o que você faz?
when: quando
where: onde
which: que, qual, quais (indica escolha)
white: branco
who: quem
wide: vasto, imenso
wife: esposa
wind: vento
window: janela
winter: inverno
with: com

wolf: lobo
woman: mulher
word: palavra
word hunt: caça-palavras
work: trabalhar, trabalho
worker: trabalhador, operário
write: escrever, escreva
wrong: errado

Y

year: ano

yes: sim
yellow: amarelo
young: jovem
you: você, vocês, tu, vós
you are: você é, você está, vocês são, vocês estão, tu és, vós sois
your: seu, sua, seus, suas, vosso, vossa, vossos, vossas
you're welcome: de nada, não há de quê (respondendo a um agradecimento)